FOREVER

THIRTEEN

A Family Tragedy
and a Young Man's Struggle to Recover
(Faith, Hope & Love)

DOUGLAS JAMES SHUMARD

Foreword by Barbara Shumard

12/14/18
Mary'
Doug Shumard

ISBN: 978-0-692-19997-8
Published by: Douglas Shumard
Printed in the United States of America
Copyright 2018 Douglas Shumard
Credit for Cover: Designed by James Hrkach
Artwork "Collision of Light and Dark" by Margaret Rose Realy,
Obl. O.S.B.
editing and interior design: Ellen Gable Hrkach

Human stories are practically always about one thing, aren't they? Death. The inevitability of death.
J.R.R. Tolkien

Acknowledgements

First of all, I thank God for allowing me to turn six pages written in 2001 into a manuscript completed some seventeen years later. I thank God for sending others into my life, at different times, but in each case a point in my life when I needed encouragement, love, and understanding.

Most importantly, to Barbara Hall Shumard, my pal, my best friend, my counselor, my advisor, my partner, and my wife for over fifty years and still counting. Had it not been for you, it couldn't be.

And to Margaret Rose Realy, Obl. O.S.B., my mentor, who provided advice and guidance over many months. She was always there for my questions, emails, or phone calls. For her assistance, I am forever grateful.

Table of Contents

Foreword

This is an honest experience of severe trauma to a young family and their children. So often we are angry, disillusioned, and devastated by what happens in our childhood. So much of our resentment, anger and grief are not understood, and so our wounds are passed to others around us, and to our children. It is the story of an eleven-year-old boy whose brother drowned in a lake during a Boy Scout outing.

Through the eyes of this eleven-year-old brother, we experience the confusion and the brokenness of all who were involved.

Recovery from the trauma experienced was hampered by a young father, James, who experienced his own trauma as a very young child. His mother walked away when he was three years old and never came back. As a very young child, he may have wondered if, maybe as a three-year-old, he was in some way responsible for her walking away.

James was compelled to be responsible, to have a good work ethic, to have high expectations to do the "right thing" as an individual, a parent, and as a member of the Catholic Church. This was perhaps in reaction to not wanting to be abandoned again and also because he was a good man.

He wanted to like himself and probably thought his success and lovability in life was dependent on how the family looked and the children behaved. Unfortunately, his eldest son did not behave that day; he was supposed to be playing baseball but wandered off with two friends to take a rickety raft on to the lake.

The day Loren died on that lake, his father James experienced loss of another family member—his wife, Helen. She was not able to turn to her husband for comfort and support; not only had she lost her firstborn son, her own mother, whom she was very close to, was hospitalized for exploratory surgery, the day before.

In this young family, the children needed to be comforted, held, and talked to. The parents were gripped not only with the current tragedy but trapped in their own wounds. Friends, family, and neighbors hardly knew what to say to them, let alone help these small children survive the loss of their brother—and the emotional withdrawal of their parents.

This story is a beautiful reminder of the graces given through redemptive suffering. Throughout his years, this eleven-year-old's experience of the death of his brother led him through severe emotional pain, a feeling of brokenness, and insecurity. He struggled with a father who was emotionally unavailable, a mother who did not initially recognize him after her emotional collapse and electro-shock treatments.

He also did not know that he had the right to be himself and not to feel burdened to be the one to take care of his siblings. His greatest asset was being a member of a family who loved and were faithful Catholics, of being educated in Catholic schools, and working through his own suffering experiences with the help of a very special teacher, Sister Rose.

Time moved on and so did the eleven-year-old boy; he became a man.

On one of our first dates in 1962, Doug asked me to

go to a drive-in movie. I do not remember the movie but will never forget him reaching into the back seat of the car and showing me his Baltimore Catechism. He wanted me to know how important his faith was. I was instantly relieved and drawn to this young man who loved God and His Church.

We married in 1964 and the family's healing began.

I loved and admired his parents and was always proud to have the name Shumard.

Barbara Shumard, LMSW, LMFT
Catholic Psychotherapy Association
National Association of Catholic Social Workers
catholictherapists.com

Shumard Family Members, 1954

Helen Clark Shumard	February 12, 1918	36
James Wilmont Shumard	March 14, 1920	34
Loren Clark Shumard	March 10, 1941	13
Douglas James Shumard	June 17, 1942	11
Dennis Michael Shumard	July 14, 1945	8
Cathy Anne Shumard	March 9, 1950	4
Thomas Lee Shumard	Sept. 8, 1953	8 mos.

Born After 1954

Jo Anne Shumard	October 8, 1957
Todd Shumard	February 14, 1962

A Trip Back In Time

"God has created me to do Him some definite service. He has committed some work to me which He has not committed to another."

~John Henry Newman

Many of us have thought of being able to visit the first home of our memory; retracing our childhood, looking back in an attempt to reconnect with the past, even if only in some small way. After retiring from Ford Motor Company in 1998, and after nearly thirty years of service, I entered the real estate business. One of the daily activities of all realtors is to review the online report of new listings.

Early one September morning, after arriving at my office, I removed my sport jacket, and carefully placed it on the back of my chair. I turned on the computer and watched with fascination as the high-speed Internet immediately came to life. I headed next to the coffee pot for the first of many cups that day. After engaging in the morning ritual of interoffice chitchat, I returned to my desk for the day's activities: reviewing and updating client files, telephone contacts, meeting schedules, and going over the latest information on the Jackson Michigan Real Estate Board website.

On this beautiful morning, there were about thirty new listings to review. The listings were typically in descending order by price and included the street address and listing realtor. As I reviewed the listings, my eyes caught a very familiar address, on Randolph St., the address of my childhood home from the time of my birth through late teens. This house brought back many memories of that home, my family, mom, dad, brothers, and sister. I recalled the good times that took place inside those walls and the very difficult times as well. I knew the importance of all that had taken place at that address and the extent to which that home, along with the people and the circumstances, had to do with the person that I had become.

There was a choice to make; I may never have this opportunity again. I picked up the phone and contacted the listing realtors who provided me with access to a house that I had not entered for nearly three decades. When we met at the Randolph address, he opened the front door, and as he was backing out of the driveway he shouted, "Don't forget to lock it up!"

My Childhood Home

As I entered the house, I was a bit apprehensive, anxious and even beginning to wonder if this was going to be the positive experience that I was hoping it would be.

770 Randolph Street

The first room I entered was what we had always called the sunroom; originally it was just a front porch. Years before, mom and dad purchased this home; the porch was nicely converted into a three seasons' room with a full roof and hinged windows on three sides, along with the original hardware that allowed my dad to hang screens in each window when spring arrived and to change the windows when winter arrived.

The sunroom is where my brothers and sister and I, along with Dad, listened to the Friday night fights; especially when one of the boxers was Carmen Basillo, who like my father was from Canastota, New York, a place that was once described as "the epicenter of Upstate New York's rich boxing heritage." We enjoyed listening to those fights and when the ringside radio announcer breathlessly told his listeners that Basillo had landed a hard left to the jaw, we all screamed with great joy. On the other hand, when that same announcer told us that Basillo took a right hand to the midsection, it was a loud "OH NO," from every one of us in the room.

Basillo held both the World Welterweight Championship, won from Tony DeMarco in 1955, and along with that, defeated Sugar Ray Robinson in 1957 to win the World Middleweight Championship. A few years after these events in our sunroom, my brother, sister and I would meet, chat with, and walk away with our hero's autograph. I must admit that I still have that Carmen Basillo autograph today.

As I continued through the sunroom and entered the hallway that separated the stairway to my right leading to the upstairs bedrooms, the living room was directly to my left. This is the room where Mom and Dad shared stories of their lives, both before and after meeting at Goodyear. They spoke of how they purchased this house in 1941 and had to put twenty dollars down in order to hold the purchase until they could get a bank loan. Mom told us over and over again how fearful she was of losing that down payment. They enjoyed telling about all of the cleaning that was required just to get to the point where they could repair, paint, carpet, and begin to furnish the house that was to be their home, and ultimately the home of Loren and I, along with Denny, Cathy, and Tom.

The living room seemed much smaller than I remembered; this was something I would feel as I continued my walk-through. I was very surprised to see that after these many years, the crown molding that dad had carefully nailed in place and painted many years ago was still there.

I was drawn back to the stairway and walked to the bedrooms upstairs. That staircase too was unchanged, still with the same hand rail and spindles of years ago. I could almost hear Dad shouting at Loren and me, "Don't run on those stairs, walk on them!" At the top of the stairs there were three bedrooms; Mom and Dad's room, Loren, Denny and I shared a room where a great many pillow fights took place, and the third bedroom for Cathy and Tom. Seven people and one small bathroom today seems like a major problem, but back then it was not the least bit unusual. All of the second-floor rooms had screened windows that provided fresh air and a gentle breeze on those hot days and evenings.

Returning to the first floor, I went into the kitchen where a number of changes had taken place, but the memories were still there. This room was not only where the meals were prepared, it was also the room where we ate all our meals, only after saying grace.

Over the years Mom and Dad put a number of coats of paint on the walls of each room. As my brothers and I grew up, we assisted in these family chores. The painting was easy enough, and in some ways, fun for Loren and I, but the younger ones required a great deal of attention to keep them from making a mess. Looking back, it was a true learning experience, because each of us as adults found painting our own homes as a relatively easy job, based on our past experience.

When Dad decided to add crown molding to our living room, we became observers. This project required something called a miter box, a tool that Dad had no experience with, and I had never heard of or saw before. We soon became aware of the importance of this tool. The boards that become the crown molding have to be cut precisely so as to hide the meeting of one board to the next. These saw-cuts could only be made with Dad's new tool, the miter box. Dad did a great job, and as I worked my way through the house, I found those miters cut boards still in place and looking beautiful all these years later.

Our basement was an old Michigan basement with a low ceiling, maybe slightly over six feet or so, and fieldstone walls painted white by Mom years ago. As I entered the basement, the same large, rotund furnace was still in place, positioned under the center of the home, and had been converted from coal to gas. There were a number of large tubes extending from the furnace to various areas of the house that you needed to duck under as you moved about in that cool damp space.

That old coal furnace was something to behold. I remember a phone conversation my mother was having, when she was requesting a ton of coke be delivered to our home. After she hung up, I excitedly ask her if we were planning a party of some sort because we had a ton of Coca-Cola on the way. Needless to say, I was disappointed to find that coke is a type of coal. The delivery of coal to our house came in a rather large heavy-duty truck, driven by a man covered in a thick layer of black coal dust from head to toe. He would attach a metal slide-like devise, known as a coal shoot, to the back of his truck. He would then open a black steel door (that at an earlier time was a basement window) and line his delivery shoot to begin the delivery of coal to our basement coal bin.

In the early 1950's, my father was employed part-time at George Bush's Store, a neighborhood grocery a block from our home. He worked full-time as a supervisor at the Goodyear plant on the other side of town, but on weekends – and occasionally during the week – he put in extra hours at the store to make ends meet. We were a family of five children, with three of us in a private Catholic school. In addition to these expenses, there were the medical bills. Dad had been in and out of the hospital for what seemed like most of my young life. Not only had he been hospitalized at our local Mercy Hospital on three or four occasions, he had also been admitted more than once to the University of Michigan and St. Joseph Hospitals, both located in Ann Arbor.

My dad was a proud man who never asked anyone for help and was determined to pay his bills. He was also a taskmaster who held the same high expectations for his children as well as for himself.

In addition to my father's illnesses, my health had not been good. Just weeks before Loren's death, I was released from Detroit's Henry Ford Hospital, where I was taken by ambulance from Jackson's Mercy Hospital because Henry Ford was the nearest facility with an artificial kidney machine (today known as dialysis). I had been diagnosed with acute nephritis and was going through kidney failure. For a number of weeks, I could not keep anything in my stomach; the only nutrition I received was via an intravenous line.

During that long ride from Jackson to Detroit, Mom sat next to me in the ambulance. I remember asking her if I was going to die. Instead of answering, she lowered her head, turned away, and sobbed.

I was admitted to the pediatric ward where I would be sharing a room with a boy about my age, whose name I remember today, Dennis Sickowicz (Pronounced Sir-co-witz).

Due to the seriousness of my illness, Mom stayed with friends in Detroit, very close to the hospital. Shortly after arriving at Henry Ford Hospital and waiting my turn for dialysis, arrangements were made for me to receive the Last Rites of the Catholic Church. When the priest entered my hospital room to discuss this, I told him that I knew what the Last Rights were and that it is for the dying and I told him that I was not going to die, and that everything was going to be okay.

One evening when Mom was in the hospital room with me, my roommate's mother was present as well. Mom noticed that Mrs. Sickowicz was rubbing something on her son's foot. Mom asked what she was doing, and Dennis' mom replied that her son was having another in a series of surgeries required due to a birth defect with his foot. She went on to say that she was applying water from Lourdes to his foot prior to the upcoming operation. She then asked my mom if she would like some for me. Mom enthusiastically rubbed the water onto my back about where she thought my kidneys might be located. She also poured a little in my drinking glass, mixing with water that was already in there. Some days later, while still waiting for dialysis and continuing with routine tests, it was found that I was in recovery and would not need dialysis. Mom, the doctors, and everyone else were convinced that this was indeed a miracle. It wasn't long before I was released and sent home.

Numerous miracles have been attributed to this water from Lourdes, where in February 1858 the Blessed Virgin Mary appeared to fourteen-year-old Bernadette Soubirous. There were eighteen visions in all. In one of those visions, the Blessed Mother told Bernadette to drink from a nearby fountain of which there was no sign of water, but of which water immediately gushed forth.

Needless to say, my hospitalization was a severe financial hardship for our family.

Five years earlier, on New Year's Day, 1948, I had been hospitalized at Mercy Hospital with Scarlet Fever. Toward the end of that same year, I was again admitted to Mercy, this time with Purpura Edema, a blood disorder. Two years prior to that, I had been admitted to Mercy Hospital with Rheumatic Fever. I had missed so much school during those years that my parents had talked to me about changing schools.

We discussed my attending what was called, "the open-air school," which my parents explained to me was a school for slow learners. I was told that this kind of school was what I needed to help me get caught up scholastically.

I remember, very clearly, that I was not at all impressed with this idea. I was happy with the school that I was attending. Many of my classmates were kids from my neighborhood. These were all friends that I would miss if I changed schools: I did everything that I could to discourage any further conversation regarding the subject of me attending a school for slow learners.

Our Dad

Dad was born in 1920 in Saskatchewan, Canada, shortly after his parents, along with his Uncle Loren and his wife Aunt Fern, each began homesteading 160 acres of farmland in that bleak desolate prairie region of Western Canada. It was 2,080 miles from their home in Canastota, New York. If they succeeded in making this acreage a productive venture, the Canadian Government would deed the land to them at no cost. During this period of time, the Canadian Government offered 160-acre parcels to any man over eighteen who would settle there. In 1901 there were only 19,200 families; fifteen years later, there were 150,300 families which included seven Shumards.

After a few years, both Shumard families realized that it was time to return to the fertile soil of their home state of New York; another 2,800-mile journey. They packed everything they owned – clothes, tools, and farm equipment – into a railroad freight car, just as they had done when left New York for Canada. As an adult,

I wish I had taken an opportunity to discuss with my father or my grandfather how they could afford those two very long trips. The train ride to Canada included four adults, farming equipment, food for the journey, and money to begin a new life. The return trip included those same things, as well as three new Shumards, my dad and his brother Charles, along with Uncle Loren and Aunt Fern's son.

Arriving back in Canastota, New York, my father's Uncle Loren purchased a farm consisting of approximately 200 acres and was very successful in his farming operation raising dairy cows and the crops to feed not only the cattle, but his family as well. My grandfather hired on as a farmhand moving from one farm to another.

My dad's mother abandoned her husband and her two sons when Dad was three years old, and his brother Charles was just a one-year-old. My dad and his brother were raised primarily by aunts and uncles since she had deserted them. To a great extent, my father raised himself, working at a very young age on farms in the Canastota area. Like many others in the 1920's and 1930's, he dropped out of school in order to provide for the family. Because of the shame he felt, he seldom discussed it and then only in hushed tones, with a reminder that this subject was never to be discussed outside our home. He was full of pride and drive, both of which may have fueled his recurring illnesses in the years to come.

When he turned seventeen, he loaded all of his belongings into a car purchased with money saved from farming and drove to Jackson, Michigan at the suggestion of a friend who had read about a tire factory that was hiring. Almost immediately, he was hired by Goodyear and was earning in one week what it had taken him months to earn as a farmhand. Unfortunately, Goodyear's minimum age requirement was eighteen. Dad had lied on his application; Goodyear found the discrepancy and had to let him go. However, in the short time that my Dad was employed, they recognized his work ethic and told him to come back when he turned eighteen. Within a matter of a few months, he returned and was rehired.

Beloved Mom

While working at Goodyear, my father met Helen Margaret Clark, who later became my mom. She came from a large Irish Catholic family. She was the second oldest of six sisters, Anna May, Angel, Donna, Connie, Pat, and Mary, and two brothers, Al and Jim. All of her brothers and sisters graduated from Jackson's St. John High School.

In 1936 she graduated from St. John High School as well. Before ever meeting my dad, she waited tables and counter at the Jackson train station; which at that time was bustling with travelers and numerous trains arriving and departing throughout the day and night. Directly across from the train station was the Otsego Hotel, which was within walking distance, and that provided a steady flow of customers for the coffee and meals available at the train station.

Mom was always proud to mention that she served coffee on many occasions to a young man named Jack Parr, a local radio announcer on Jackson's WIBM who came in often after his shift ended. He was born in

Canton, Ohio, and later moved to Jackson as a teenager. After WIBM he worked for Detroit's WJR as a humorous disc jockey.

You may remember Jack Parr as one of the three best hosts of the "Tonight Show." Steve Allen was the host from 1954 to 1957. He was followed by Jack Parr from 1957 to 1962, and in 1962 along came Johnny Carson from 1962 to 1992.

In 1937 Goodyear opened a new plant in Jackson to begin production of tires and tubes. Mom took a job with Goodyear and in a matter of a three or four years it wasn't automobile tires and tubes, but armament for the war effort. Goodyear was producing fuel tanks and Mom was a chief inspector for these self-sealing fuel tanks.

Once she met James Shumard, she says it was love at first sight for both of them; they married in 1940 and the rest is history.

My Home Parish

I have great memories of my home parish. It was the first parish in the world to be named, "Queen of the Miraculous Medal," established in 1934 by the Vincentian Fathers headquartered in Germantown, Pennsylvania. The first priest I remember is Father John H. Dougherty C.M. (Congregation of Missions), who served as Assistant Pastor from 1934 to 1947, and then as Pastor until 1956. Although he was the third pastor serving this parish, he was instrumental in leading our parish through some challenging financial times. He was a dynamic leader who was responsible for our building a beautiful new church and saw his parish grow from 140 families to over 800 families, which increased school enrollment to over 600 students.

My very first memory of going to Mass was when I was about five years old and maybe four feet tall. At that time we were in the "basement church" which required us to go down a dozen steps to enter the relatively small sanctuary. I could hear the prayers, the singing; smell the burning candles and the rich aroma of incense. But, because of my lack of height, and still true for kids today, I could only see the back of the suit coat worn by the gentleman in the pew in front of me. I asked my parents to allow me to sit on the end of the pew on the main aisle so that I could see what was going on at the altar. I noticed a couple of teenagers who walked down the aisle with the priest as mass began. I was very curious about what they were doing to help the priest and wondered if that would be something that I could do someday.

Fr. John Dougherty, C.M.

Fr. Doc, as everyone called him, was a great man and a great priest. He was a big, imposing Irishman with a stern face and a gruff voice. He was a hero to the adults and feared by the boys of the parish. All the altar boys, me included, were panic-stricken when we found that we were serving Mass for Fr. Doc. We knew if we made the slightest mistake during Mass we could be reprimanded on the spot, "in front of God and everybody" as the saying goes.

It was not possible to escape his reprimands, even if you were not an altar server. That opportunity was available to all students on report card day. Father's usual procedure was for him to walk into the classroom wearing his black suit, black shirt, black shoes, and starched Roman collar going from one classroom at a time, through the entire school to personally present each student with his or her report card. This experience made the altar boy reprimands look like a walk in the park! He began by saying a few words of encouragement to all the kids in the class. The girls sat smiling, with hands folded in front of them, eagerly awaiting their usual outstanding grades. I sat there, like many of the boys in my class, hoping this day would just go away.

After his words of encouragement were spoken, the Dominican Sisters who were our teachers would hand him the stack of report cards. He would then call out our names to individually step forward to receive the card. By the time we reached the front of the room where he stood, he had reviewed all grades on our card, both academic and for classroom behavior. For those who did well, he had a pat on the head, a kind word, and a twinkle in his eye. For those who did not do so well, the twinkle in the eye turned into an angry stare, the kind word into a sometimes less-than-friendly diatribe, and the pat on the head was nowhere to be found.

On at least one occasion, he expressed his disappointment in me by asking how I could take grades like these home when my father had been so sick. He ranted and raved about what a disappointment I was and how I had let them down. This public calling out, in the presence of our classmates, was never a pleasant experience for those of us who struggled in school. This was also difficult for the Sisters who were our teachers. It was obvious, on occasion, that even they were concerned with his behavior.

Fr. Francis White and Fr. Louis Lawler shared duties with Fr. Dougherty. Both were soft-spoken and easy to talk with, both in and out of the confessional. Fr. White was our Boy Scout chaplain, and also served as baseball umpire at the annual seventh- and eighth-grade baseball games.

Fr. Lawler was the most devout priest that I ever served for. When he began saying the consecration prayers, (in those days, it was a Latin Mass) Fr. Lawler pronounced each word slowly and clearly, more so than any other priest. Sister Jeremias, our altar server trainer, explained to us that Fr. Lawler was a relatively new priest, and he knew that the words of the consecration, both over the host and over the wine, must be recited exactly as written. With this information, I paid closer attention to other priests and found that they did much the same.

Fr. Dougherty died of a heart attack in May 1960 at the age of 71, leaving a significant legacy of a parish that began with less than 200 families in its first year, to nearly two thousand families today.

Father Dougherty at Our Door

*"Kind words can be short and easy to speak, but their echoes
are truly endless."*
~St. Teresa of Calcutta

Saturday May 1st, 1954, early spring in Jackson,
Michigan, warm for that time of year, blue sky and
sunshine with a long-anticipated summer just ahead. It
was mid-afternoon, and my eight-year-old brother
Dennis and I were in the backyard trying to decide
what to do with the rest of the day. Our older brother,
Loren, had left the previous day for a weekend Boy
Scout outing. Our younger sister Cathy had just
awakened from her afternoon nap and was with
mother in the kitchen.

Denny, Doug and Loren

I could hear my mother through the screen door leading from the backyard to the kitchen, talking to my aunt on the phone. Both my mother and aunt were very concerned about their mom, my grandma, who had gone into Mercy Hospital just the day before for a number of tests. Based on what I was overhearing, my grandmother was going to require surgery. I had no idea what the problem was, other than that she had been experiencing stomach pains and the doctors were unable to provide any relief or diagnosis. Mom and her sister agreed to meet at the hospital the following day to visit her. As my mother was hanging up the phone, Tom, the baby of the family, was beginning to cry as he awakened from his nap. I could hear Mom walking up the stairs to bring Tom down to the kitchen.

My father was working his part-time job at George Bush's Store, a neighborhood grocery just a block from our home.

On this first day of May, less than a month after my release from Detroit's Henry Ford Hospital, I was feeling great. As a matter of fact, I was very disappointed that my parents had not let me go on the Boy Scout outing that particular weekend with my brother Loren. Instead, here I was with my younger brother in the backyard. Our backyard was small, about twenty feet square and enclosed with a secondhand wire fence that dad had picked up from someone he worked with at Goodyear. Denny and I were in the yard, not far from the corner of the house. I was looking through the fence toward the street at the front of the house when I noticed my dad's friend, Larry Ambs, driving faster than I had ever seen anyone drive down Randolph Street. He made a fast right turn onto South West Avenue without even slowing down for the stop sign at the end of our street. I couldn't help but yell to my brother, "Wow! Denny, did you see that?"

Within a few moments, I saw Mr. Ambs again. Still driving fast, but this time coming from the opposite direction, he came to a screeching stop at our curb. No longer able to see the car, I heard its doors open and close. I heard the doorbell ring through the screen door leading to our kitchen, not far from where we were standing. My mother answered the front door and seeing Fr. Dougherty and her friends Larry and Helen Ambs, she realized that this was not a social visit. I could hear her say, "Father Dougherty, what's wrong? Tell me what's wrong."

It was later that I realized that Mr. Ambs had driven past our house the first time on his way to pick up Father Dougherty.

Father Dougherty, our church pastor, walked into the kitchen with Mr. and Mrs. Ambs. I couldn't remember Father Dougherty ever being in our home before. He did visit my dad during his many hospitalizations and had visited me during some of my stays in the hospital, but I was sure this was the first visit to our home.

The Father Dougherty who stood in our kitchen that day was one I had not experienced before. His presence was imposing as always, but his eyes expressed a concern and love that I had not seen before. His usual booming voice was filled with compassion and hope as he broke the news to my mother. I can remember Father Doc explaining to my mother that Loren was missing, but that while the situation was serious, there was hope. This was followed by a great deal of confusion, praying, crying, and ringing phones; then the sounds of someone running. As I turned, I saw my father running through our neighbors' backyard, running faster than I had ever seen him run. While nearly at full speed, he placed a hand on one of our fence posts and leaped over the fence into our yard. Without noticing Denny or I, he raced into the house. More conversation, more crying, more phone, calls, and mass confusion.

Before long, Mr. Ambs and my father left to go to Camp Teetonkah, the Boy Scout camp located on Wolf Lake about 20 minutes east of our home. My father wanted to be there as the search continued. The two of them arrived at the camp and found it closed; Dad and Mr. Ambs were unaware that this particular scout outing was not taking place at Camp Teetonkah, but rather at a private farm some eleven miles south of our home. They returned home heartbroken and extremely upset that they didn't know where the boys were – they had gone to the wrong place.

Within an hour or so of my fathers' return, we received official word that Loren had indeed drowned. Loren was thirteen years old for only six weeks. His birthday was March 10th. My 12th birthday would be on June 17th, only six weeks away; we were just fourteen months apart. My parents' oldest son was dead, my brother was dead, and one of my heroes was gone.

At some point during all the confusion and sorrow, I remember realizing that I was no longer the second oldest of five children. I was now the oldest of four. I knew how much I looked up to Loren, how much I watched his every move, how much I always wanted to be like him. I now felt a responsibility to my brothers and sister. I felt that I had to be to them what Loren was to me. I remember saying to my mother as I went to bed that night, "Well, I guess I'm the big brother now." Mom just nodded and began to cry again.

I had no idea then that I was creating a monumental and totally impossible challenge for myself.

Front Page News

"The scars that you can't see are the hardest to heal."
~Astrid Alauda

The next morning I still remember very clearly. I remember it because that day started just as the prior day had ended: with feelings of devastation, tears, and confusion. As I mentioned earlier, Dad was a proud man who never asked anyone for help, and he held high expectations for his children as well as for himself. Loren and I both caught onto that way of life, and of course, wanted to please our dad. I just assumed that I would be delivering the Sunday newspaper that morning. As I was getting dressed to deliver the paper route, Mom came into my room; she was still crying. She appeared to have been awake all night. Between the tears, she announced that she would come along with me; maybe to try and find some normalcy and to get away from the confusion.

I could see the door to my parents' bedroom was closed, with that room's light visible between the bottom of the door and the floor. I could also hear Dad sniffle and sob as he passed the floor of that room. I think my dad too needed some time alone.

At 5:30 a.m., Mom and I pulled out of our driveway to get a head start delivering Loren's paper route; after all, I was Loren's substitute whenever he needed me, and today I was needed. Mom and I had eighty-four papers to deliver, after which we would attend our regular nine a.m. Sunday Mass along with the rest of the family.

The sun was just coming up as we arrived at the corner of Fourth and Griswold, the pick-up point where bundles of newspapers were dropped off for the five or six paper carriers to pick up and begin their daily deliveries. All of the bundles were marked with a number, designating which bundle belonged to which paper carrier.

After I cut the twine that secured the bundle of papers for Route 243, the next step was to remove the scrap newspapers on top of the bundle, placed there to protect the papers that we were about to deliver from the elements. This is when I would, for the first time, read that shocking headline: "BOY SCOUT CAMPER 13, DROWNS AS RAFT SINKS." I was startled, and Mom was shocked and upset to see in bold print the death of her son. It was not only a front-page story but the headline! Alongside the story was the picture taken for the same newspaper one year earlier. That picture showed Loren with the biggest smile you ever saw because he had just won the local soapbox derby.

Loren had turned twelve shortly before the Jackson, Michigan, Coaster Classic (Soapbox Derby) was held. When the competition was announced, months earlier, both Loren and I had registered as participants. We both sought out sponsors who would finance our projects in exchange for their names being prominently displayed on the sides of the racers. With the supervision of our sponsors and our dad, we built our racecars.

12-Year-Old Wins Coaster Race

A crowd of about 1,500 braved heat and sunburn to see 12-year-old Loren C. Shumard, 770 Randolph St., capture the fifth annual Junior Chamber of Commerce Coaster Classic Sunday. The race was run on the special blacktopped course down the west side of the Cascades hill. Sixteen boys competed in two classes.

Douglas Shumard, 11-year-old brother of the winner, won a trophy for having the best engineered car in the race.

Earnest Hilton, 11, of 403 Homewild, was given the best sportsmanship trophy because he offered the cable from his car to the driver of another car that had broken down. The offer was declined. Ernest is recovering from a recent illness. He had to diet to lose 8 1-2 pounds to pass the weight limit so he could race. His illness was not due to dieting.

Jack Bassar, 13, of 636 Oak St., was the runnerup.

For winning the class B contest, Loren received a bicycle and trophy and for taking the best of three heats from Bassar, winner of the Class A contest, Loren received a $100 defense bond. Loren won the first heat; Bassar was disqualified in the second heat for getting out of his designated lane, and Loren came back to win the third heat. His average time for the day was approximately 31 miles an hour.

He was sponsored by Curran's Friendly Service, 1205 S. West.

Miss Susan McGee, Coaster Classic queen, started the race and bestowed a kiss on the cheek of the winner to wind up the day's program.

The awards were presented by John Worthing, chairman of this year's event.

—Citizen Patriot Photograph.

A WINNER SMILES—Loren C. Shumard, 12, of 770 Randolph, is happy because he won the 5th annual Junior Chamber of Commerce Coaster Classic Sunday afternoon. After capturing Class B honors, he bested Jack Bassar, 13, of 636 Oak St., Class A winner.

THURSDAY, JUNE 25, 1953.

—Citizen Patriot Photograph.

L SET—Douglas Shumard, 770 Randolph, gives his coaster a thorough check in preparation r .ne Junior Chamber of Commerce Coaster classic on the Cascades hill Sunday.

35

It was a big day for both of us when the June, 1953 event arrived. Loren and I eventually raced against each other for the championship in our division. He won, and then moved up to race and defeat the other division champs to take home the overall championship.

For winning the championship, he took home a trophy, a $100 Savings Bond, and a new bike. I took home a trophy and a $50 Savings Bond for best-designed car. That was a great day for both of us. I was proud of him, he was proud of me, and our parents were proud of us. Everyone was smiling.

No one was smiling now. My mother and I were about to deliver a Sunday morning newspaper to eighty-four subscribers, announcing the death only twelve hours earlier of her son, my brother, and their newsboy. Those readers of the Jackson Citizen Patriot on Route 243 on that May morning, would, over their morning coffee, read about the death of their newspaper boy. Some would read in disbelief and have a fleeting sense of grief for our family, take a sip of coffee, and move on to the sports page. Others may have abandoned the front page and moved to the society section of the paper.

For Loren's family, for the scouts who were with him, for the scout leaders, and for many of his classmates, it would be much more difficult. For many, it took days and months to grieve. For others, it took years. Some never completely moved on.

I think the idea on that Sunday morning was to try to keep the day as normal as possible. By six a.m. it was becoming obvious, even to an eleven-year-old, that our lives would not be normal for some time to come.

Our parents always accompanied us to Sunday and Holy Day Masses and saw to it that we went to Confession most Saturday afternoons, which too was often a family affair. Mom and Dad were faithful and devout Catholics, and they were dedicated to ensuring that their children would follow in the faith. This Sunday morning, nine a.m. Mass would be no exception. A neighbor had volunteered to watch over four-year-old Cathy, and eight-month-old Tommy in our home. Mom, Dad, Dennis, and I were seated about halfway back in the church.

As Mass continued, we were all standing as the priest began the prayers for the sick and recently deceased of the parish. When the name of my brother was announced as one of the recently deceased, I could hear gasps from around the church. It had been, after all, only about fifteen hours since the news broke, and many of our family's friends were not aware of the terrible accident that occurred the prior day.

Of all the gasps that were heard at that moment in that church, on that Sunday morning none were more noticeable than my mother's. As common as it was for those announcements to be made at that point in the Mass, I am sure that my mother never expected to hear the name of her own son, even on this morning. A shiver that turned into shaking accompanied her gasp, as she tried to cover her face with both hands. My father placed his arm around her as she began to sob.

At about one p.m. that afternoon, we all went to Cavanaugh Funeral Home for a private family viewing. This was a very difficult time for all of us. I suspect that my father had to identify Loren's body the prior day, but he never said, and I never asked. Regardless of whether he had seen Loren's body earlier or not, both he and my mother were severely shaken.

Finally, as we all stood at the casket, my mother commented on how nice Loren looked in his white shirt, bow tie, and new plaid jacket. Only a few weeks earlier, I had kidded Loren about his "Spike Jones" jacket that was red, green, yellow, and blue plaid. He had purchased it for a school dance and was proud of it; he received a number of compliments wearing it, and he knew that he looked great in it.

As I stared at him in the casket, I remembered the huge smile on his face each time he put that jacket on. I remembered the smile on his face the day that he won the Soapbox Derby. I remembered all of the times he smiled. I noticed that he was not smiling now. And, for the first time, I didn't agree with my mother: I didn't think he looked "nice." He didn't look nice at all.

Mom was rubbing Loren's hand as she was crying. When she noticed that I was watching her, she told me that I could touch his hand, that it would be okay. Finally, I touched his hand and squeezed his arm. His hand was very cold, and his arm was very hard. There were too many good memories of a very alive Loren that I wanted to remember, rather than what I was seeing and what I was being asked to touch at that moment. I wanted to remember Loren as I knew him, as he was, and not as I saw him then.

The Newspaper Story

From the Jackson Citizen Patriot, Sunday May 2, 1954

BOY SCOUT CAMPER, 13, DROWNS AS RAFT SINKS

Pal Risks Life, But Try Fails

Loren Shumard, Troop 24, Dies as Weeping Companions Pray

A week-end outing for Boy Scout Troop 24 was tragically interrupted Saturday afternoon when Loren Shumard, 13, son of Mr. and Mrs. J.W. Shumard, 770 Randolph, drowned a short distance from the troop's campsite.

Loren and two companions, Jimmy Dwyer, 13, of 702 Sixth, and John Dragonetti, 14, of 1925 W Michigan, were playing on a raft in a small lake on the property of Douglas MacCready 9126 Myers Rd. about 11 miles southeast of Jackson. Suddenly the raft sank, throwing the boys into about 15 feet of water.

All three boys started swimming for shore after Loren called to his companions that he was all right. The Dragonetti youth said he turned back a moment later and saw that Loren was sinking. He said he swam back and grabbed hold of Loren twice but was unable to hold him up. He then made a third attempt to rescue him but was unable to find him.

WON COASTER CLASSIC

Loren, who won the Junior Chamber of Commerce Coaster Classic last June, was one of 30 Boy Scouts from troop 24 who were camping on the side of a hill overlooking the small lake.

William McCarthy, 763 W. Washington, the scoutmaster, and John Lindburg, 1503 Warren, the assistant scoutmaster, were directing a softball game in

39

a nearby field when they heard the shouts of a small group of boys who had wandered down by the lake.

Both men sprinted to the scene and immediately dived into the water in an effort to find the boy. They were aided by Mr. MacCready, the owner of the property, but were unsuccessful.

The sheriff's department and the Summit Township fire department dispatched boats and grappling hooks to the scene. And as they dragged for the body, a group of Boy Scouts with tear-stained cheeks knelt and prayed.

FOUND AFTER 30 MINUTES

At about 5:30 p.m. some 50 minutes after Loren sank from sight, the body was recovered by Sheriff Deputies Max Green and Jesse Shanks and State Trooper Donald Kaiser. The Rev. Fr. Francis White said the last rites of the Catholic Church while coroner Loren Bates was being summoned.

The troop outing, which began Friday and was scheduled to end Sunday, was over. The scouts slowly rolled up their blankets, folded their tents and shuffled back to the bus that would return all but one to his home.

Loren's death was the second drowning in Jackson County that year. The first occurred on Palm Sunday when the infant son of State Trooper Alfred Torrey drowned in Gillett's Lake.

MANY MISFORTUNES

The death of the Shumard youth is another in a series of misfortunes that have plagued the Shumard family. A couple of years ago, his father suffered a prolonged illness and was hospitalized for months. Recently, Loren's younger brother, Douglas, had been in Ford

40

Hospital in Detroit for a serious illness. It is reported that Mr. Shumard has been working an extra job to pay hospital bills.

Loren is survived by his parents, three brothers, Douglas, Dennis and Thomas; one sister Cathy Anne; his grandparents, Mr. and Mrs. Alfred Clark and James L. Shumard, all of Jackson.

The body has been taken to the Cavanaugh Funeral Home.

JACKSON, MICHIGAN, SUNDAY, MAY 2, 1954.　★　HOME EDITION　PRICE: SEVEN CENTS DAILY. TEN CENTS SUNDAY.

Boy Scout Camper, 13, Drowns as Raft Sinks

Wind Rips Meeker, Oklahoma

Town Nearly 'Wiped Out' by Torando; Many More Lashed.

BULLETIN.
Meeker, Okla. - (AP) - Residents, forewarned, ducked into storm cellars Saturday when a tornado struck this town, 30 miles east of Oklahoma City, and no deaths were reported. Twenty-six were injured.

Oklahoma (AP) - A vicious string of tornadoes wiped Oklahoma Saturday, nearly "wiping out" the town of Meeker and battering 12 other communities with an untold loss of life and property.

Two persons were known dead and 9 others injured, but scores were reported hurt in the storm at Meeker where a pall of silence existed because of knocked down communications.

Police at Shawnee 18 miles south of there, said they had a call from Meeker for "all help possible—our town is nearly wiped out."

Ambulances, nurses, doctors and emergency help was rushed to the area and first reports at Shawnee said the injured from Meeker were filling the three hospitals there.

OTHERS ENROUTE.

Others injured were enroute to Oklahoma City, 30 miles east. Meeker, a community of 1,000 persons, is known as "the home of Carl Hubbell," famous New York Giant baseball pitcher.

FIREMEN JOIN IN SEARCH — Sunbeit Township Fire Chief Duane Harrington (center) and two firemen prepare to launch a rescue boat and join sheriff deputies and state troopers (on lake) as they drag for the body of Loren Shumard, 13, of 770 Randolph, who drowned Saturday afternoon while on a Boy Scout outing.
—Citizen Patriot Photograph

Pal Risks Life, but Try Fails

Loren Shumard, Troop 24, Dies as Weeping Companions Pray.

BY RON MILTON

A week-end outing for Boy Scout Troop 24 was tragically interrupted Saturday afternoon when Loren Shumard, 13, son of Mr. and Mrs. James W. Shumards, 770 Randolph, drowned a short distance from the troop's campsite.

Loren and two companions, Jimmy Dwyer, 12, of 702 Sixth, and John Dragonetti, 14, of 1925 W. Michigan, were playing on a raft in a small lake on the property of Douglas MacCready, 6156 Myers Rd., about 11 miles southeast of Jackson.

Suddenly the raft sank, throwing the boys into about 16 feet of water.

All three boys started swimming for shore after Loren called to his companions that he was all right. The Dragonetti youth said he turned back a moment later and saw that Loren was sinking.

He said he swam back and grabbed hold of Loren twice but was unable to hold him up. He then made a third attempt to rescue him but he was unable to find him.

WON COASTER CLASSIC.

Loren, who won the Junior Chamber of Commerce Coaster Classic last June, was one of 20 Boy Scouts from Troop 24 who were camping on the side of a hill overlooking the small lake.

William McCarthy, 763 W. Washington, the scoutmaster, and

Power Co. Awaits Full | **Decision Up to People Wednesday** **Officials Call Sewer**

...ll Sewer
Important

A. HOVING.

y Hall Reporter.)

ric leaders term "one of the
ckson history comes up Wed-

approve a charter amendment

answer those questions in a series
of three articles beginning today.

CONTROL GROWTH.

City officials and those who keep
close tab on civic progress say
that a city is no bigger than its
sewer and water lines. Any community that is lacking in either
or both can not add new houses,
business firms and factories.

This in turn stifles a city—hits
it hard economically. Without new
industries and business there are
no new jobs. And the property
valuation of a city does not in-
crease much, depriving residents
of either a tax reduction or an in-
crease in municipal services.

There is another angle: Over-
loaded sewers lead to a serious
health hazard. No epidemic of
disease resulting from basements
flooded with sewer filth has oc-
cured in Jackson. But health au-
thorities say the city is on the
verge of serious health trouble.

Thus the election Wednesday is
considered a key to Jackson's fu-
ture.

PERIL PROGRESS.

Mayor James N. House says:
"This city is on the way to going
places. We are doing things and
building things. But they may not
be of much value if Jackson is
forced to halt this progress because
of lack of sewers."

Harold D. Miller, chairman of
the Greater Jackson Assn. "citi-
zens committee for adequate sewers," says: "Jackson is at the

(Continued on Page 2, Column 2.)

DROWNS — Loran Shumard
wore this smile after he won
the Junior Chamber of Commerce Coaster Classic last
June. Loren died Saturday afternoon when he became Jackson county's second drowning
victim of 1954.

William McCarthy, 163 W.
Washington, the scoutmaster, and
John Lindberg, 1503 Warren, the
assistant scoutmaster, were directing a softball game in a nearby field when they heard the
shouts of a small group of boys
who had wandered down by the
lake.

Both men sprinted to the scene
and immediately dived into the
water in an effort to find the boy.
They were aided by Mr. Mac-
Cready, the owner of the property,
but were unsuccessful.

The sheriff department and
Summit township fire department
dispatched boats and grappling
hooks to the scene. And as they
dragged for the body, a group of
Boy Scouts with tear-stained
cheeks knelt and prayed.

FOUND AFTER 50 MINUTES.

At about 5:30 p. m. some 50
minutes after Loren sank from
sight, the body was recovered by
Sheriff Deputies Max Green and
Jesse Shanks and State Trooper
Donald Kaiser. The Rev. Fr.
Francis White said the last rites
of the Catholic church while
Coroner Loren Bates was being
summoned.

The troop outing, which began
Friday and was scheduled to end
Sunday, was over. The Scouts
slowly rolled up their blankets,
folded their tents and shuffled
back to the bus that would return
all but one to his home.

Loren's death is the second
drowning in Jackson county this
year. The first occurred on Palm
Sunday, when the infant son of
State Trooper Alfred Torrey
drowned in Gillett's lake.

MANY MISFORTUNES.

The death of the Shumard
youngster is another in a series of
misfortunes that have plagued the
Shumard family. A couple of year
ago, his father suffered a prolonged illness and was hospitalized
for months. Recently, Loren's
younger brother, Douglas, had
been in Ford hospital in Detroit
for a serious illness. It is reported
that Mr. Shumard has been working at extra jobs to pay hospital
bills.

Loren is survived by his parents;
three brothers, Douglas, Dennis,
and Thomas; one sister, Kathy
Ann; his grandparents, Mr. and
Mrs. Alfred Clark and James L.
Shumard, all of Jackson.

The body has been taken to
Cavanaugh funeral home.

VanFleet To Survey East

Honolulu -(P)- Gen. James A.
VanFleet arrived by plane Saturday on his way to the Far East on
a survey as special representative
of President Eisenhower with the
rank of ambassador.

VanFleet, his wife and W. J. Mc-
Neill, assistant secretary of de-
fense, planned to remain in Honolulu until Monday.

VanFleet said present plans do
not call for him to visit Indo-China,
but he indicated that changes
"might develop."

Funeral Home

"Yesterday is gone. Tomorrow has yet to come. We only have today. Let us begin."
~St. Teresa of Calcutta

Monday would be the last full day for our family to be at the funeral home. The day before had been a long and tiring day for my parents. It had been slightly over twenty-four hours from the time Father Doc had announced to my parents that Loren was "missing" to the time that our family was standing at the casket greeting friends and family.

On Sunday there was only a single visitation period for the public that lasted from 5 to 9 p.m. This day, Monday, would be an even more demanding day with two separate visitation periods, the first from two p.m. to four p.m. and the other from six p.m. to nine p.m.

Along with our neighbors and members of the parish, many relatives from the area were there with us for most of that two-day period. They included my mom's six sisters and two brothers; along with many of my cousins, my Grandpa Clark (Grandma Clark was still in the hospital), and my Grandpa Shumard. In addition to the many relatives from Jackson, other relatives were arriving from out of town, Mom's aunts and uncles from Ohio and Dad's relatives from New York and Pennsylvania. Everyone from both sides of my family were in the room during those two days to share our grief, except for my mother's mother, who would have surgery before the end of the week.

In addition to relatives, many neighbors, including State Representative George Bassett and Jack Curran,

43

the sponsor of Loren's car in the Soapbox Derby, were among the first to arrive. There were close friends of my parents, including Dr. Holst, who brought Loren into the world, and Dr. Stone who had been Loren's pediatrician. There were people my Dad worked with, including the Goodyear plant manager, E.T. Ruffner. There were people who we knew only in passing such as the Bassar Family, whose son Jack was the runner-up in the Soapbox Derby that Loren had won the year before. Even total strangers came by to express their sympathy. Many visited the funeral home more than once during the Sunday and Monday schedule. Teens and pre-teens, boys and girls, seemed to outnumber adults. They included kids from our neighborhood, classmates of Loren's and kids with whom Loren had played Midget Football.

Members of the Boy Scout troop, including Jim Dwyer and John Dragonetti, who were with him on the raft when it sank, came to the funeral home together. I saw the wives of the three scoutmasters at the funeral home, but I didn't see any of the scoutmasters.

Most, if not all, of the nuns from Queen of the Miraculous Medal School were also there.

On this very same day, Monday, May 3, 1954, the Jackson newspaper published the following:

Shumard Boy's Rites Set Tuesday

Services for Loren Shumard, son of Mr. and Mrs. James W. Shumard, 770 Randolph, will be held at 10 a.m. Tuesday in the Queen of the Miraculous Medal Church, with internment in St. John's Cemetery. The 13-year-old boy drowned Saturday during a weekend outing of Boy Scout Troop 24.

Members of the Scout troop will attend the services in a group and several will be honorary pallbearers.

The drowning happened in a small lake on the property of Douglas MacCready, 9124 Myers Rd., about 11 miles southeast of Jackson. Loren and two companions were playing on a raft, when suddenly, the raft sank, throwing the boys into about 15 feet of water. His two companions swam to safety after one of them had tried to save the drowning boy.

PARENTS NOT CRITICAL

In talking with officials of the Jackson Boy Scout Council, parents of the boy have freed them of any blame or criticism because of the accident. They said: "Loren had always been a very active boy and loved his scouting activity. He was a good swimmer, having gone to the Council Boy Scout camp two years and has taken many overnight camping trips with his troop."

"His troop leaders have all done fine work with the boys and we know they are absolutely blameless in this tragic accident. It was just one of those things and we are so appreciative of the fine time Loren had in scouting. It is wonderful training for the boys."

Scout Executive Montford Mead, commenting on the accident, said that it is the first time in his 25 years' experience, and the first time in the history of the Land O' Lakes Council that a fatal accident had happened during a scouting activity.

Mr. Mead pointed out that the basic policy of the Boy Scouts of America is to do everything possible to train boys by experience in the safest and best methods of camping and in all other outdoor activities. He estimated that in the history of the Land O' Lakes Council as many as 60,000 boys have gone camping three or four times a year without a serious mishap.

On the other hand, throughout the country thousands of former scouts, who are now adults, owe their lives and the lives of companions to the knowledge and skills acquired in scouting.

Mr. Mead said that every Boy Scout Council in America strives constantly to use the latest and best methods in order to provide their volunteer leaders with proper methods. However any accident is thoroughly studied to prevent its recurrence.

NEWSPAPER BOY

Loren was a Citizen Patriot carrier boy, assigned to Route 243, which includes Fourth St., High St. between West Ave. and Fourth St. and the edge of the Jackson Mound addition. He is survived by his parents; three brothers, Douglas, Dennis and Thomas; one sister Cathy Anne; his grandparents, Mr. and Mrs. Alfred Clark and James L. Shumard all of Jackson.

both air strips.

Shumard Boy's Rites Set Tuesday

Services for Loren Shumard, son of Mr. and Mrs. James W. Shumard, 770 Randolph, will be held at 10 a. m. Tuesday in the Queen of Miraculous Medal church, with interment in St. John's cemetery. The 13-year-old boy drowned Saturday during a week-end outing of Boy Scout Troop 24.

Members of the Scout troop will attend the services in a group and several will be honorary bearers.

The drowning happened in a small lake on the property of Douglas MacCready, 9124 Myers Rd., about 11 miles southeast of Jackson. Loren and two companions were playing on a raft when, suddenly, the raft sank, throwing the boys into about 15 feet of water. His two companions swam to safety, after one of them had tried to save the drowning boy.

PARENTS NOT CRITICAL

In talking with officials of the Jackson Boy Scout council, parents of the boy have freed them of any blame or criticism because of the accident. They said:

"___ ___ ___ ___ ___ a very active boy and lived his scouting activity. He was a good swimmer, having gone to the council Boy Scout camp two years, and has taken many overnight camping trips with his troop.

"His troop leaders have all done fine work with the boys and we know that they are absolutely ___ ___ ___ accident ___ ___ just one of those things and we are so appreciative ___ ___ time Loren had in scouting. It is wonderful training for boys."

Scout Executive Montford Mead, commenting on the accident, said (Continued on Page 2. Column 6.)

Scoffs at Recession

---

2. Roy M. Cohn, general counsel

Shumard Boy's Rites Set Tuesday

(Continued from Page One.)

that it was the first time in his 25 years experience and the first time in the history of the Land O' Lakes council that a fatal accident had happened during a scouting activity.

Mr. Mead pointed out that the basic policy of the Boy Scouts of America is to do everything possible to train boys by experience in the safest and best methods of camping and in all other outdoor activities. He estimated that in the history of the Land O' Lakes council as many as 60,000 boys have gone camping three or four times a year without serious mishap.

On the other hand, throughout the country thousands of former scouts, who are now adults, owe their lives and the lives of companions to the knowledge and skills acquired in scouting.

Mr. Mead said that every Boy Scout council in America strives constantly to use the latest and best training methods in order to provide their volunteer leaders with proper methods. However any accident is thoroughly studied to prevent its recurrence.

NEWSPAPER BOY

Loren was a Citizen Patriot carrier boy, assigned to Route 247 which includes Fourth St., High St. between West Ave and Fourth St. and the edge of the Jackson Mound addition.

He is survived by his parents; three brothers, Douglas, Dennis and Thomas; one sister, Kathy Ann; his grandparents, Mr. and Mrs. Alfred Clark and James L. Shumard, all of Jackson.

Trainmen

Newspaper Article May 3

47

Two days before this article was published, Loren had drowned, and his parents are quoted as saying, "His troop leaders have all done fine work with the boys and we know they are absolutely blameless in this tragic accident. It was just one of those things and we are so appreciative of the fine time Loren had in scouting. It is wonderful training for the boys."

Mom and Dad were both upset and very disappointed to read that piece. They had no idea where those statements came from.

The Funeral

"God had one son on earth without sin, but never one without suffering."
~St. Augustine

That Tuesday was the most difficult of all days that we had faced since the news of Loren's drowning. The funeral Mass was not scheduled until ten a.m., but we left the house by 8:30. It was just a few steps out of our back door to our garage, and then a couple more steps to the car. As we took those few steps, we all noticed it had turned cold overnight. It had been in the high 70's and low 80's since Friday, but that morning was gray and overcast, with bone-chilling cold.

The drive from our house on Randolph Street to the Cavanaugh Funeral Home was only a mile, but it was a drive that we had taken (what seemed like) a dozen times over the past two days. I was glad and thought this would be our last.

I was ready for it to be over. I wanted to get back to our normal life again. I wanted to have a meal that my mother prepared, not a meal consisting of tables filled with food prepared by many different, but well-meaning, neighbors. I wanted us all to sit together at the same table, telling stories of what happened at school, what was taking place in the neighborhood, or what was going on in the factory where Dad worked. At that point, I would even have settled for my father raising his voice at Dennis or me for using one of his tools and failing to put it back where it belonged.

I wanted something, anything, that resembled our

usual, normal existence.

Somehow my eleven-year-old mind didn't register that it would never be the same again. It would not even be normal again.

We were, naturally, the first to arrive at the funeral home. As we walked inside the brightly-lit room, the recorded organ music and the smell of flowers once more overwhelmed me. Flowers bordered both sides of the casket, from the floor to the ceiling and six feet deep. Flowers lined each of the walls as well. It looked like everyone in town had sent flowers. They were everywhere, they were all very beautiful, and I remember how much they meant to my parents.

No matter how beautiful they were, no matter how much they meant to my parents, no matter how significant they had been to the sender, I would never again be able to smell a flower without remembering my brother's funeral.

That beautiful aroma represented a terrible loss.

It wasn't long before the room was filled to overflowing. There was a brief ceremony, conducted by Father White, the Boy Scout Chaplain, who was also the Assistant Pastor of our parish. This was then followed by a procession to Queen of the Miraculous Medal Church.

The church was only two miles from Cavanaugh Funeral Home. My mother and father, my brother Denny, and I would ride in a long black Cadillac. Mr. Cavanaugh drove the car while my mother and father sat in the roomy back seat. My brother and I rode in the jump seat, the seats that unfolded from the back of both front seats, thus accommodating additional passengers. The car carrying our family would follow another black

Cadillac that contained the casket that held my brother. A police motorcycle escort would lead the quarter-mile-long procession the two miles to Queens.

As we left the funeral home parking lot, the lengthy procession eventually turned onto South West Avenue, and we would be within sight of our home on Randolph. I knew this would be especially difficult for my parents because of the fact that Loren would never be coming home again. I watched my mother closely as we approached the turn onto South West Avenue. The instant that my mother caught sight of the back of our home she broke down and began to cry. My father held her close to him as he struggled to keep back his tears.

Once again, I wanted to cry, but I remembered all of the times that I had been told, "Don't bother your parents. They are going through a lot right now." I didn't want my crying to make them any more upset than they already were. I was finding that I was struggling less and less with holding it back; it was getting to be easy. Soon I would find that even when I wanted to, even when I needed to cry, the tears would not be allowed to come.

As our lengthy procession approached the church, it became obvious that a great many people had driven directly to the church and had not been part of our procession. Cars were already parked in every available space, for what seemed like blocks, around the church. I had never seen so many cars and so many people at our church at any time before; so many parishioners, friends, relatives, neighbors, and even total strangers who truly cared and were grieving along with us.

The funeral procession was directed to a reserved

51

parking area while the cars carrying my brother's casket and our family, were parked directly in front of church. As we got out of the Cadillac, six of Loren's friends approached the hearse. These six would be the pallbearers. As they began their preparations to carry Loren's casket into the church, a group of uniformed scouts began forming two lines about eight feet apart, leading from the hearse to the front door of the church. The casket carried by the pallbearers, our family, and everyone still outside the church would pass through this honor guard leading from the curb.

As we followed the casket down the aisle into the already-crowded church, the finality of it all began to set in. Even though I knew that we would be going to a graveside service after this requiem Mass, I still looked at this service as the final step, the end of organized services surrounding this terrible event. I was sure that when this day was over, we could at last start to get back to normal; that word normal, what an interesting word, so short, but so full of warmth and comfort. As I sat in that pew in the front of our church, as the service began, my mind wandered to what had been normal for Loren and me.

This was my brother's funeral, my best friend's funeral. My thoughts were of the wonderful times we had together. Wonderful because we were young, we had a loving family, we had friends and at that age we only knew fun. We didn't know anything about real problems. To us, a problem was not being able to get enough kids together for a ballgame.

Memories of Loren

Loren and I were altar boys together at Queen of the Miraculous Medal Parish. He had been serving Mass for a full year before I started. As a beginner, I was assigned to a more experienced server, as a partner/trainer, who would serve Mass with me. Fortunately, I was assigned to Loren. His patience with my Latin pronunciation, especially with the longer prayers like the Confiteor, added to my confidence. Because of my brother, I was capable, excited, and proud, to be an altar boy for many years to come. We were altar boys together; we played together and fought together.

One summer day, we were staying overnight at our grandmother's home on the other side of town. There was a big tough kid who lived next-door. He had called Loren a terrible name and said he was going to "kick his butt." Even before he had finished talking, he had jumped on my brother and wrestled him to the ground. He was on top of Loren with both knees on Loren's shoulders, so that Loren couldn't move. He was about to take a swing at Loren when I jumped onto the pile. All I did was knock him off my brother, but that was all that Loren needed was to get his arms free. Before long, the kid from next door was headed home, holding his bloodied nose. Loren thanked me; then we had a great laugh together. I had never been in any kind of fight before, and I don't think my brother had either. We both knew, that day, that we would always be able to depend on each other.

In the summer, we used to lie on the damp cool grass, wearing our usual blue jeans, white T-shirts, and high-top black tennis shoes. We lay with our hands cupped behind our heads, our eyes skyward and a dandelion stem between our teeth and discussed our futures. We never used the word adult in our conversations; we never talked about turning twenty-one or even eighteen. We talked about those things that we wanted to do when we "got big." "I want to join the Air Force and fly airplanes when I get big." Funny, we never thought about being adults, only about being big. Even today, when I look at the green grass on a warm summer afternoon I am reminded of those carefree conversations.

In addition to the obvious sights that remind us of things from the past, to this day, there are sounds and aromas that bring back memories. For instance, a burning candle, no matter where I am when I smell it burning, takes me back to my days as an altar boy, as does the aroma of wine. Loren created a number of subtle sound memories for me. I remember most vividly an early Sunday morning; it must have been 5:30 when Loren had gotten up to dress for his paper route. I was only half-awake, the light in the bedroom that I shared with Loren and Denny was off, and the room was dark except for the light reflecting into our room from the half-opened bathroom door where Loren was brushing his teeth.

Even lying in bed in that semi-awake state listening to him brushing, listening to the different sounds as the brush worked on the front teeth and then the back with the sounds changing as the lips then came together or apart for the front teeth and back. I remember his muffled footsteps as he came back into our room, still leaving the lights off so as not to wake Denny or me. I remember the sound of his shirt sliding off the hanger and the hanger swinging back and forth on the clothes closet bar. I remember the sound that his blue jeans made as he wiggled his legs in and the sound of his belt being worked through the loops. Most vivid in my memory is the sound of him tying his shoes in that still dark room. I could hear him pull the tips of the wax shoe laces tightly then pull the laces at each eye, pull again at the tips, then begin to form the loops and wrap tightly into a finished bow.

Loren was just fourteen months older than I. As might be expected, we were very close, but like all brothers, we had our fair share of minor disagreements. Loren was someone I looked up to. He was popular in school and was obviously smart and quick to catch on to, even the most complicated things.

He was talented with his hands. I watched in admiration as he built and painted a three x four locker out of discarded orange crates. At first, I was afraid he was making it to lock his prized possessions away from me. I remember how thrilled and proud I was when he showed me where he had hidden the key to that chest. His purpose was not to keep me out as I had feared, but only to have a safe spot for his prize possessions, away from the prying fingers and destructive hands of our younger siblings.

I tested his trust in me at the first opportunity. While he was away, involved in one of his many activities, I sought out that key, unlocked and opened the chest to see what treasures it contained. The excitement of that experience was similar to being turned loose in a toy store, alone, for an unlimited time, to examine in detail everything on the shelves.

All of his treasures were neatly arranged: a two-inch

stack of baseball cards held together with a rubber band, a pile of comic books including Archie, Little Lulu, and Superman. There was a baseball, torn at the seam with a piece of leather the size and shape of my ear, pulled away from the now-exposed windings of the ball. It was obvious, only to a couple of pre-teens, that this baseball had a lot of games left in it. I also found his new ball mitt that was the envy of every kid in the neighborhood. He was especially proud of that glove because he had purchased it with money that he earned on his paper route.

In another corner of the chest was a coffee can filled with marbles. He could shoot marbles much better than I and better than most of the other kids on the block, so he was always adding to that coffee can marble collection. The footlocker also held some of his Boy Scout equipment including a mess kit that contained a frying pan, dinner plate, drinking cup, knife, fork, and spoon, all of which fitted one inside the other to make a compact package that fit into a small canvas bag.

The majority of space in that chest was reserved for the real purpose of the footlocker and that was to hold his collection of cap pistols along with a large collection of cap pistol parts. Loren was the guy to see when you pulled the trigger on your cap gun and the hammer didn't respond. In addition to building the footlocker with his own hands, he was the local cap gun repairman. WHAT A BROTHER!

Loren at Scout Camp

Loren Clark Shumard
1941 – 1954

The fifties were a great time to grow up; there was always something to do. Very little was organized; we improvised and made it up as we went along. Our mothers were busy at home all day, so we knew someone was there if needed and we also knew someone was watching, needed or not.

Our activities included baseball, football, kick-the-can, hide and seek, and badminton in good weather. When it rained, we played checkers, Monopoly, Chinese checkers, and other indoor activities. These indoor activities could take place in almost any home in the neighborhood. In every case, there was a mom at home. In the winter months, it was sledding, ice-skating, building snow forts, and having snowball fights.

Our sporting equipment and toys were interesting. Typically there was only one kid in the neighborhood who had a good baseball or decent bat. Most of our baseballs, for example, had stitches that were worn and torn. The kid down the street had a good one.

My bat was secondhand and had been broken and repaired by my dad with white glue and a couple of screws. I still remember the sting of that repaired bat when contact with the ball was made. The kid across the street had a good bat.

My football had been left in the rain and a hunk of the black rubber bladder, about the size of an egg, stuck through the football webbing. The kid in the next block had a good one.

We all loved to see who could jump for the longest time on a pogo stick. There was only one pogo stick in the neighborhood, and we all got to used it. The point is, we shared. Everyone had something, no one had everything, few of us had the same things, and yet all of us had fun.

Our ball games were played everywhere except in ballparks. We played in the street until one of our mothers saw us, and then we moved on to the many open areas surrounding where I lived. There was a county park, the Cascades, less than two blocks from our neighborhood. We used this same field for football, baseball, hitting golf balls, and sledding in the winter. For a baseball game, we used broken tree branches or hunks of tree bark for bases; sometimes we used our shirts or jackets instead.

I especially loved baseball. I am left-handed, and with most everything, my baseball mitt was a hand-me-down from my right-handed brother. I got to be known as the "fastest gun in the west" because I could catch a fly ball, with that glove on my left hand, grab the ball with my right hand, toss off the glove from my left hand, grab the ball from my right hand and throw with my left hand into the infield nearly as fast as a right-hander using the same mitt.

My brother shared many things with me but none more important than his patience. When I first played baseball with him and his friends, I was not yet able to catch a fly ball. As hard as I might try, when that ball landed in my glove, it would always find some way of falling to the ground before I could squeeze it firmly in my glove. This happened on such a regular basis that as I stood under a pop-up waiting to make the catch, I could hear the shouts of, "Keep running. He's never going to catch it."

It was Loren who would tell me what I was doing right and what I needed to do to improve. Finally, one day the pop-up came my way. I heard the comment, "Keep running. He's never going to catch it." This time the ball stuck in my glove like it had glue on it. My brother was as happy as I was and was the first to slap me on the back, giving me one of his big smiles. I don't ever remember dropping a ball after that first real catch. Life was simple. We were young and growing up with lots of friends, and we had each other.

He was my brother, we were having fun. What could possibly go wrong? It was 1954.

What Could Go Wrong?

"Pray as if everything depended on God and work as if everything depended on you."
~St. Ignatius Loyola

What could possibly go wrong had gone wrong. I was now sitting in the front row of the church where Loren and I had been altar boys together, the church where we had attended daily Mass most school days of our lives. I was sitting with my brother Denny and my parents, within a matter of feet from a shiny metal casket that contained my brother who I had been allowed to see for the very last time, at the funeral home, less than an hour earlier.

I have almost no memory of the funeral service itself. However, I remember after the service very well. Loren's casket, flanked by the pallbearers, led our family and the rest of the congregation, up the aisle and out of church. As we passed through the church doors to the outside, we noticed that, not only was it much colder, but also it had begun to snow. We were all quite surprised. After all, it was May 4th. How could it possibly be snowing when, only a few days before, the temperature had reached eighty-two degrees?

As we stood on the sidewalk waiting for the casket to be placed back into the hearse, I heard Mom say to no one in particular, "Loren would have liked this. He loved snow." I remember thinking that Loren would have loved sunshine too. He would have loved rain. Weather meant nothing to him; it just didn't matter. I also knew that Mom knew that too, and her comment was just something that a mother would say, something that you would say about someone you loved that could be made to fit the situation, regardless of whether it was rain, snow, or sunshine. Maybe it was simply an attempt to express some sort of feeling, regardless of the words.

At about the same time, the cold wind blew through my light sport coat and I began to shiver. We had left our home hours before and had given no thought to wearing coats on this May morning. I suddenly felt someone's coat being placed across my shoulders over my sport coat. It felt good; not only the warmth of the coat, but I could feel the warmth left behind by the person who had just taken it off and given it to me. Jo Ann Smith (Mrs. Mel Winn) a very close family friend had once again provided me comfort.

The cemetery was less than a mile from Cavanaugh Funeral Home. We would retrace our earlier route back toward the funeral home and on to St. John's Cemetery. Once again, we turned from South West Avenue onto High Street passing just behind our home. As the procession, led by the police escort, made the left turn under the red light, with traffic stopped and lined up in all directions, Mom said, "Look, they're all stopping for him now. They never stopped for him before."

This was an intersection that Loren, Denny, and I had crossed many times before. Traffic was heavy here, but none of us had ever been involved in any accidents, or even near-misses. I wasn't sure exactly what my mother meant. I put this comment in the same category with her earlier comment about Loren loving snow; another attempt to try to find some meaning.

I had never been to St. John's Cemetery before. The section toward which we were headed was a rolling parcel of land, with many tall and well-established trees. We pulled up in front of one particularly large oak. Next to that tree was what appeared to be a pile of dirt, covered with a blanket of artificial grass which was now partially covered with freshly fallen May snow. Next to that pile was a small canopy that covered two dozen or so chairs neatly arranged around a low platform on which the casket was placed.

I was glad that I had been given that coat on the church steps because it would be quite a few minutes before everyone could get in place for this final service to begin. Although the snow had stopped, it was still cold and everywhere we looked, there was a light groundcover of snow.

After the casket was put in place and all of the family and friends were gathered around, the service began. It was a very brief service, especially compared to the others that we had been involved with over the prior two days.

I remember only two other things about the day of my brother's funeral. We ended up at my grandparents' house at the end of that long day. My Uncle Al had the radio turned on to WJR, a Detroit radio station. Bob Reynolds, the station sportscaster, was talking about the day's thirty-one-degree temperature, with snow and ice that had been responsible for the cancellation of the basketball game between University of Michigan and Notre Dame scheduled to be played that day in Ann Arbor, only forty miles away.

I also learned that evening why I had not seen my grandmother during those difficult four days. She was scheduled for surgery that very evening. The stomach problem that she had been experiencing had not responded to treatment, and it was hoped that this operation would help the doctors find a solution. My grandmother's surgery took place the night Loren was buried. I was later told that the doctors found cancer. There was little that could be done for my mother's mom.

On Monday, May 10th, my grandmother, my mother's mom, died. She was only 59 years old. She had been told of her grandson's death earlier in the week. Needless to say, Mom was devastated; especially because her mother's confinement in the hospital had prevented her being with her own daughter and family at this tragic time. What a terrible, awful time that must have been for my mom, two devastating deaths within nine days.

Mom was in a complete state of shock. Her son had drowned on May 1st, and now, just days later, her mother was dead. Another funeral, another three days of mourning, another two days at Cavanaugh Funeral Home, another funeral Mass, and another graveside service.

Noise in the Night

"Spread love everywhere you go. Let no one ever come to you without leaving happier."
~St. Teresa of Calcutta

It was late May, a warm Friday evening; or maybe it was early morning. I really don't remember. I do remember that it was 'the middle of the night'. I was asleep in my room, which I shared with Dennis and Loren, before...

There was a late spring storm, thunder, and occasional lightning, and rain began to fall. The rain blowing in through the open window wakened me. As I got out of bed to close the window, I heard muffled sounds that I associated with the storm. As I returned to bed, those sounds I now recognized as a loud conversation between my parents, not an argument but more of a pained discussion. My mother was telling my dad that she needed to get away; she wanted to go to her Uncle Joe's quiet, peaceful cabin in northern Michigan. It was used by her brothers and sisters – my aunts and uncles – at various times during the year.

My dad had taken Loren, Denny, and me there the previous summer. There were only two things that I could remember about that cabin. One was that when we went to Uncle Joe's home to get the keys to the cabin, he had said something about having swept dirt under the rug in the kitchen when he cleaned up the last time he was there. We all laughed, thinking that was the best joke we had ever heard. When we arrived and moved our belongings into the cabin, we noticed a lump under the rug. Sure enough, there in all its glory, was the pile of dirt that Uncle Joe had swept under the rug.

The other (and most memorable) memory of that visit was that there was no indoor toilet. There was an outhouse, complete with a half-moon on the door, a toilet paper roll hanging on a nail and a stink that I had never experienced before. I refused to go near that thing, until about the third day when I thought I was going to explode and no longer had a choice.

With what I could remember about Uncle Joe's place, I couldn't imagine why anyone, especially my mom, would want to go there. Regardless of my memories, my mother was insisting that she be allowed to go, alone and immediately. My dad was just as insistent that she not go, that she "get herself together," and take care of her family.

As the discussion continued between my parents, my four-year-old sister Cathy began to stir in her room, which was situated between my bedroom and my parents' room. Cathy shared her room with our baby brother, eight-month-old Tom. I didn't want Cathy to wake up Tom because the discussion between my parents would be interrupted. I'm not sure why I felt any obligation. Maybe it was that new responsibility that I had of being the big brother now. I had that feeling again, that I had to be, to my brothers and sisters, what Loren had been to me, a hero, a caretaker, a leader, someone to look up to.

Whatever the reason, I went into Cathy's room, picked her up, and walked the floor with her until she fell asleep again. I put her back in bed without waking Tom and more importantly, without my parents being disturbed. As I returned to my room, I noticed that the conversation stopped, and as I glanced at their bedroom door, I could see that the light had been turned off.

The next morning, a Saturday, was not too unusual, everyone going about his or her business as usual. Dad had gone to his weekend job at George Bush's Grocery Store, Mom was a bit withdrawn, but I didn't think much about it based on the conversation that I had overheard the evening before. I didn't even think about mentioning the fact that I had heard their conversation. They would have been embarrassed and, worse yet, they would not have wanted to include me in any of that.

Since Loren's death, there had been absolutely no conversation between any of us about the death, the circumstances, or the other people involved. There had never been any discussion about how I felt, how they felt, or how we would get through this.

I had always thought we were a fairly typical family. We were a good family, a loving family, a religious family, and a close family, but now we were coming apart. Everyone was dealing only with himself or herself. We were not helping each other. We were all going in different directions, pushing as hard as we could, to force all of our feelings and desperation back inside and as deep into our gut as possible. I was afraid to ask questions or look for help because I kept being told by concerned friends and neighbors, "Don't bother your parents, they are going through a lot right now."

If they were all so wise as to know what my parents were going through, why didn't someone know what my brother and sister and I were going through? Why was (is) the assumption that kids don't have feelings, and that kids don't understand?

So on this Saturday morning, with everyone else going about his or her business, I went about mine. I had papers to deliver and route collections to take care of. This was the day that I made the rounds to collect payment from my customers, a task that usually took over an hour. By the time I finished collections, it would be time to deliver the papers, and I'd walk the route all over again.

Doug

The corner of Fourth and Griswold was a fairly busy intersection in Jackson. There were two gas stations at this intersection and one of those was on the corner where the Jackson Citizen Patriot dropped the newspapers that Loren used to deliver, and that was now my responsibility. Ted Keys was the owner/operator of the Cities Service Station, a very clean, but busy one-man operation.

There were usually three or four other carriers waiting for the truck to drop our bundles of papers. While we waited, it was standard practice to go into Ted's station and buy a bottle of pop, a candy bar, or a bag of chips. Any of these items could be purchased for a nickel. That sounds cheap now, but believe it or not, it wasn't every day that we could afford any one of these items. This was collection day, so I had money enough for one of each.

When Ted's service business was slow, he was happy to have our nickel business. When he was busy with mechanical repairs, working with a car up on the lift, he was sometimes not very excited about coming into the station, wiping the grease from his hands and retrieving a candy bar from his display case or a bag of chips from the rack behind the counter. Nothing was in a machine, not even the pop. The cold drinks were in a cooler, half-filled with cold water that might have been ice at one time, but we were never quite sure. If Ted was really busy, or had a difficult day, he would ask us to leave and not bother him, sometimes politely, sometimes not. We always did as he asked, but we were back the next day to bless him with our nickels.

When the papers arrived, it was time to go to work. Our papers were wrapped with heavy twine, an old newspaper on both the top and bottom of the bundle to protect the current day's papers from the elements. I didn't always have my pocketknife with me, so if one of the other carriers had his, I borrowed it to cut the twine that secured my bundles. If no one had his knife on that particular day, we pulled on the twine as hard as we could and moved it back and forth, in a sawing motion, generating enough heat on the twine for it to smoke and eventually snap. We removed the cover papers from the top and bottom of the bundles, wrapped them tightly with the twine that we had removed, and tossed them in a burning barrel behind Ted Keys City Service Station.

After folding some of my papers and stuffing them in my bag, I began my short walk to the beginning point of my paper route. As I walked, I folded the rest of the newspapers so that as I arrived at each customer's house I could flip the paper to the porch without missing a step or slowing down. I had eighty-four customers and it normally took me an hour or more to make my deliveries. I was always looking for a more efficient track to improve my timing and once set a personal record of only forty minutes to deliver the complete route. Unfortunately, achieving this record didn't allow me time to retrieve those papers that missed the porch and landed in the bushes. The telephone complaints that I received on that record-setting day taught me that keeping the customer happy was more important than giving myself fifteen minutes spare time.

On this particular Saturday, I was pleased with myself. I had been a good big brother the night before and carried off my new responsibilities fairly well, I thought. I took care of my sister until she fell back to sleep. I didn't let her wake the baby. Most importantly, my mom and dad's conversation had not been disturbed. I was sure that, whatever the problem was, they had worked it out. I was feeling good but beginning to wonder if being the big brother brought more responsibility than I really wanted.

I worked my way north on the west side of Forth Street, then back on the east side of Fourth to High Street. West on High Street to Mound, south on Mound to Randolph, then across the street and north on Mound to High Street and again west on High Street to South West Ave. There was only one house on South West Avenue, before I turned east on my own street, Randolph. Our home was the second one from the corner, and even before I got to the corner, I saw the ambulance. It was right in front of my house; the big door on the rear of the ambulance was opened, and I could see that it was empty. There were no attendants inside and the stretcher was gone.

I ran to the house, dropped my newspaper bag on the sidewalk and raced inside. In the living room, my dad and my aunt were standing near the couch. As I got closer, I could see that my mother was lying on the couch. She was very still and quiet. She was breathing, and her eyes were opened so I knew she was alive. I couldn't figure out why she didn't blink. She was motionless, unable to speak, eyes wide open, but unable to blink. She was looking right at me, but I could tell by the look on her face that she was not seeing me.

As I stood there alongside my father and aunt, neither of them acknowledged my presence; neither paid any attention to the fact that I was a witness to this event. I was frightened and confused. Life was not getting back to normal as I had hoped. Just the opposite, unbelievably, things were getting worse. We were drawing further and further apart. Even though my mother was less than three feet from me, she was, in reality, a million miles away.

My father on the other hand, although present, active, and aware, was completely withdrawn and non-communicative with my brother and me. He never spoke to us about Loren's death; not about how it happened, about his feelings, about our feelings. I was made to feel that it was a subject that was never to be opened; it was a subject that was too painful for him to discuss. I know what his pain was. I know how difficult it would have been for him to talk about it because I know how painful it was for me. What I was most sure of was that I needed to talk. I needed to ask questions. I needed to feel like someone knew that I was there. I needed to be acknowledged.

Most importantly, I needed someone to tell me that it was going to be all right. I needed someone to tell me that they understood my feelings, that they cared, and that our family would get through this.

I thought back to the previous evening when Mom and Dad were having the discussion about her wanting to go to Uncle Joe's to "get away." I had originally thought that Dad had talked her out of it, but now as my mom was being gently lifted into that ambulance and taken to the hospital, I was wondering if maybe she was getting away after all.

My mother, within a ten-day period, had experienced the death of her oldest son and the death of her mother.

Within that same ten days, I had lost my brother and my grandmother. During that same period of time, my father had been distant at best and non-supportive at worst. Now my mother was gone. I never felt so alone. I had to talk to someone. I needed someone to talk to. Even though there was a telephone in the house, I was not comfortable making a call with my aunt in the house. I went to the corner phone booth about a block from the house and phoned the convent to talk to one of my teachers. After finding the number in the phonebook, I dialed without knowing what I was going to say. I realized even then that what I was going to say wasn't why I was calling. I was calling because I hoped that someone could help me, so that someone would finally say to me that everything would be all right, that somehow our lives would come back together.

I was calling to speak to Sister Rose Augustine. Sister Rose had spent a lot of after-class hours talking to me and trying to help me through the past few weeks. The phone into the convent only rang two or three times before it was answered. I recognized the voice immediately. It belonged to Sister Jeremias, the most feared of all the sisters at Queen of the Miraculous Medal School.

Sister Jeremias was a stern, tough, no-nonsense sister who seldom smiled and who would be the last person I would go to for help. I asked to speak to Sister Rose and was told that she was in chapel. I knew that you couldn't interrupt a sister in chapel for any reason but, before I could say anything else, Sister Jeremias recognized my voice and asked if she could help. I wasn't going to turn down an offer for help, even from my least favorite sister. I proceeded to spill my guts. I told her that my mother was just taken to the hospital. I told her how my mother had looked when I walked into the room. I even told her that my mother couldn't blink. I told her that I wanted her and the other sisters to pray for my mom.

As I spoke the words, "Please pray for my mom," I began to cry. I tried to hold it back like I did at my brother's funeral when Mrs. Wright, our next-door neighbor, told me repeatedly that men don't cry. Be strong for your parents as they are going through a lot right now. Mrs. Wright was not there now, my parents were not there now, and I cried. I cried hard and I cry now as I remember that terrible experience, that terrible day, that terrible event.

As hard as I tried, I couldn't hold it back. I talked and cried, cried and talked. This was the first time that I could remember crying. Not when we were told Loren had drowned, not at the funeral home, at the funeral Mass, and not at the cemetery. At first, I was embarrassed to talk to Sister. At first, I was embarrassed to cry, but then all of the sudden, it felt good to talk, and even more surprising, it felt good to cry.

Sister Jeremias was kind, patient, and understanding. She listened to all that I had to say and offered me comfort. She promised me that she and the other sisters would immediately begin praying for my mom and told me to call back if I needed to talk again.

I felt better as I left that telephone booth but, as I retrieved my newspaper bag to complete my deliveries, I began to once again feel the enormity of the situation. *Would things ever get back to normal?*

A Private Hospital

*"Find out how much God has given you and from it take
what you need; the remainder is needed by others."*
~St. Augustine

It was early the following week, when my dad told
me my mother was going to be transferred from Mercy
Hospital, our local Catholic hospital, to a private
hospital near Ann Arbor. He went on to tell me the
name of that hospital was Mercywood Sanitarium. He
quickly explained that Mercywood was a hospital for
those who had become exhausted and were having a
tough time dealing with problems in their lives. He told
me that I might hear people refer to that place as a
hospital for crazy people, and that I was to pay no
attention to them. He told me that those people were
being cruel and didn't understand the sickness being
dealt with in that hospital.

My dad was right. For a long time, even before my
brother's death, I had heard lots of kids refer to
Mercywood as a hospital for crazy people. He was also
right that those who spoke of it in those terms did not
understand the illness being dealt with there.
Unfortunately, he was most correct about the cruelty of
people, because even those who didn't speak the word
crazy would say it in many other ways, with both their
words and their body language.

It wasn't until much later that I learned that my
mother's staring off into space, not focusing and not
blinking, was something called a catatonic state. Worse

75

yet, I was told that the reason she was taken to Mercywood was because she had experienced a nervous breakdown. I was not too sure what a nervous breakdown was, but I knew what the other kids had always said about Mercywood.

Dad realized that he needed help, because of his full-time job at Goodyear, his part-time job at the grocery store, and his household responsibilities with four children to care for.

My Uncle Jim and Aunt Louise had been married for a short time and had been house hunting; Dad came to an agreement with them that they could move into our home expense free, in exchange for maintaining the house and preparing the meals, as well as caring for Cathy, Dennis and me. Prior to this, a family friend had volunteered to take my brother Tom into their house, until Mom could come home.

The arrangement seemed to work out fairly well for a while. Jim and Louise were newlyweds, and after a brief period of time, they began to show some frustration. After all, rather than it being just the two of them spending 24/7 together alone, they were responsible for three children ranging in age from four years to a preteen.

Still, it was a dramatic change from the usual family routine. We didn't have Mom, and I wondered how long it would be before she could come home; how long would it be before we would be a family again.

Mom's formal diagnosis was depression. I am sure that my dad found that no more comforting than the words "nervous breakdown." As for me, I had no idea how serious this diagnosis really was.

My mother was hospitalized from the end of May

through the end of September, much longer than the twenty-seven-day average in which the hospital administration took such pride. During that time I received limited information regarding her illness, either directly from my dad or by overhearing conversation with various relatives. I knew, for example, Mom was depressed and that she was unable to deal with Loren's death. I learned that the solution to her depression and inability to deal with my brother's death was something called shock treatments. We became accustomed to hearing, simply, "treatment," as in, "I wasn't able to see your mother today because she had a treatment."

All I knew at the time was that these treatments were intended to make my mother forget the painful memory of my brother's death. At the time of Loren's death, I was one month away from my twelfth birthday, but even at that age I thought an electric shock, designed to make a person forget, was a bit extreme.

Mom received shock treatments on Monday, Wednesday, and Friday. The way that she knew a treatment was coming was when she received only black coffee before breakfast. The treatment had to be given on an empty stomach, so prior to treatment, when her breakfast consisted of only black coffee; she knew that dreaded treatment was only minutes away.

During the course of her stay, Mom received at least thirty-five electroshock treatments. The shock treatments were successful in alleviating her depression, but at the cost of the loss of a great deal of her memory.

I remember Dad taking Denny, Cathy, and me to

Mercywood to visit Mom. Visiting hours were two p.m. to four p.m. and seven p.m. to eight p.m. Tuesday, Thursday, Saturday, and Sunday. I don't remember how many times we went to visit, but I do remember visiting. The hospital was a rather plain-looking, long, three-story brick building. The grounds were a bit more imposing. There was a tall six or eight-foot wire fence surrounding the eighty-acre facility. On the day of our visit, a number of patients were enjoying the large grassy courtyard area. I remember wondering how these patients would be able to walk anywhere with that tall fence, coupled with the fact that they all moved almost as though they were moving in slow motion. I concluded, at the age of twelve years, that because of that big fence, they knew there was no place to go, so they were in no hurry. Later, I would realize that the real reason they moved so slowly was because they were heavily medicated.

I was so looking forward to that first visit. I saw at it as a major step in our getting back to normal, in getting back to being a family again. Most importantly, we would finally have our mother back. I looked at that visit as a sign that she was close to coming back home. I waited on a hard-wooden bench outside on the hospital lawn while my dad went to Mom's room to bring her to see me. As my dad and my mom were walking down the hospital steps coming in my direction, I noticed that Mom looked very serious. No smile, not much expression at all. I knew that when she spotted me, her expression would change. I had not seen her in months. I was sure that she missed her family as much as we missed her. I was even surer that when she caught sight of me, there would be hugging and kissing and maybe even some crying, just like in the movies.

As they got closer, she seemed to look right at me, but she never made eye contact. I noticed that she was still glancing around; even though I was sure she had seen me. Even when they were within only a few yards of me, she still didn't seem to see me. Not until she was right in front of me did we finally make eye contact. There was still no change to her expressionless face.

At that age, I didn't know anything about the effects of medication or shock therapy. What I did know was that my own mother had no idea who I was.

Eventually Mom returned home. She had to become reacquainted with her own family. She didn't recognize her own children; she didn't know her best friends. She got lost walking around the neighborhood where she had lived for fourteen years. She was unable to function in her own kitchen. She had no idea what to cook or how to cook.

My single hope during all of these painful months had been for someone to wrap their arms around me and say, "Everything will be all right; everything will soon get back to normal." I was beginning to realize that things would not only never get back to normal, but that the definition of normal would take on an entirely new meaning in our household.

We had lost our brother, we had lost our grandmother, and now, even though she was home, we had lost our mother. In addition to that, I was setting my identity aside and trying to be Loren, trying to be the big brother and the eldest son. I was trying to be the person that I had imagined Loren to be. I was trying to be the son that I thought my parents had seen in Loren. Whoever I was, I was being set aside as I tried to become someone else. My father had withdrawn from the family and retreated to his work, both in the factory and in his part-time job. Our house was becoming just a building filled with strangers.

Seven months after Loren's death

In a 1965 newspaper article, Mercywood was described as "a solid example of what can be done to overcome the insane-asylum mystique, which still tends to surround society's conception of mental hospitals." This reference to insane asylum is strikingly similar to, and possibly a bit more crude than the irreverent, childish term that we used as kids; a hospital for crazy people.

Some days, possibly weeks after the funeral, one of our neighbors came to the front door and ask to talk to

Dad. Mom was in Mercywood at this point, so it was just the two of them, but I was in an adjoining room where I couldn't help hearing most of their conversation.

This neighbor was a well-established attorney and was trying to convince Dad to file a lawsuit against the many parties that he viewed as possibly culpable. It was a lengthy, very polite back and forth, with my father holding firm to not file suit.

I was proud of Dad then, and I am proud of him now for that decision. I never asked him any questions regarding this issue; nevertheless, as I have thought about it in recent years, I know that he was ashamed of Loren for his actions on that fateful day. Dad wanted above all else to get this tragedy behind us, rather than lengthening our grief by dragging it out for many more weeks, months, or even years in courts. Also, I think he possibly looked at this as blood money earned by people who profit from tragedy.

Sister Rose Augustine, O.P.

"We ourselves feel that what we are doing is just a drop in the ocean. But the ocean would be less because of that missing drop."
~St. Teresa of Calcutta

Sister Rose Augustine O.P. was a member of the Dominican Sisters, a worldwide religious order that was founded in France in the thirteenth century by St. Dominic. Each sister bears the initials O.P. after her name as a sign of her vow in the Order of Preachers, the formal name of the Dominican Order.

Sister Rose was my seventh-grade teacher when school began the September following Loren's death. She also had been my teacher in the fifth grade; therefore, she knew me well. Sister Rose was an outstanding teacher and was one of the most dedicated, loving, caring people I have ever encountered.

Sometime after Loren's death, I was kept after school about once a week, by Sister Rose, to discuss various subjects. I had no idea, in the beginning, why she kept me after school so often, but after a while, it became obvious that she was concerned about how I was dealing with the loss of my brother. During our after-school sessions, she sat behind her desk while I sat on a chair on the opposite side.

I remember vividly how she looked behind that desk. In 1954, all Dominican sisters wore a white habit. The veil and wimple from the top of the head to the shoulders, exposed only a portion of the face; mid-forehead to just below the chin. The ears and hair were never seen.

The white tunic extended from her neck to just above the top of her black shoes. Even her arms were covered. This left only her hands and face exposed. The white wimple was then topped with a black veil extending from the top of the head and down the back to waist level. Her face was perfect! Clear, smooth, and very white; I remember thinking that the sisters probably didn't get very much sun.

Our meetings always started with the same conversation. Sister Rose would ask me, "Well Douglas, how are you doing?" My response was always the same, "I'm doing good, Sister, how you doing?" She would smile and then say, "No, really, how is it going with you? How is everything at home?" I might respond with something about a recent visit to my mom at Mercywood or, during another meeting, how Mom was doing after she returned home.

We discussed what it was like when Mom came home from the hospital and walked around the house looking like she had never seen the inside of that home before. We talked about how Mom sometimes seemed to be only pretending that she recognized us, her own children. We discussed the possibility that maybe some of the medication that she took may have affected her memory. We discussed the shock treatments and the effect that may have had.

During one of our many after-school meetings, Sister Rose opened the subject of me wearing Loren's clothes. She suggested that wearing Loren's clothes might not be such a good idea. She pointed out that it might not be good for my mother to continually see Loren's clothes day after day. She also suggested that it might not be good for me either.

During the 1950's, in working-class families, it was common practice to pass down clothing, toys, sports equipment, etc. from one sibling to the next, as each of those items were outgrown. Our family was no different. When I outgrew my clothes, they naturally went to my younger brother, Dennis. Before Loren's death, I received his hand-me-downs on a regular basis. I had always accepted those items with great pride; I could gauge my growth based on the frequency with which Loren's shirts, jeans, socks, and shoes came my way. I always wanted to be like Loren: smart, athletic with many friends (especially girls). Receiving his clothes had always been some small step in catching up with him, a way of getting closer to being just like him. I received all of Loren's clothes after he died. I had always received and worn his hand-me-downs; therefore, I didn't see anything unusual in wearing his clothes this time.

Sister Rose may never have known how important these sessions were to me. There was absolutely no conversation at home regarding the subject of Loren's death. There was no conversation regarding how anyone was doing to cope with this loss. The subject was completely ignored. More than just ignored, it wasn't allowed.

My father wouldn't allow us to talk about Loren. I thought at the time that the reason was that it was just too painful for him. I didn't really believe that, but I couldn't think of any other reason. I even remember a brief conversation between my dad and mom shortly after she came home from Mercywood. As I mentioned before, due to the numerous shock treatments she had received, Mom had a difficult time remembering many things. During this particular conversation, she asked my dad something about Loren's death. Dad's response was, "I will answer your question, but I don't ever want to discuss this subject again."

Sister Rose was there for me. She was there when I needed her most. More importantly, she was there when I didn't even know that I needed her. I will forever be grateful to Sister Rose Augustine (Gloria Kiefer).

Sister Rose Augustine, O.P.

The *Ad Altare Dei* Medal

"I will not say, do not weep, for not all tears are an evil."
~J.R.R. Tolkien

I don't remember ever considering dropping out of the Scouts after Loren's drowning. Looking back, I can't imagine why I didn't drop out, or for that matter, why my parents didn't insist that I not belong. For whatever reason, I continued.

Not only did I continue with scouting activities, I did it wearing Loren's scout uniform and using his camping gear. I was proud to wear those clothes, and I never thought anything about it.

Late in 1956, a little over two years after Loren's death, two scouts from our troop were selected to work toward meeting the requirements for a Boy Scout/Catholic Church Award, called the *Ad Altare Dei* Medal (English translation, To the Altar of God). I was selected along with my friend, Leo Lyng. We were told that, when we completed the requirements for the award, Bishop Joseph H. Albers, Diocese of Lansing, would present the awards to us during a ceremony at Sunday Mass.

There was no doubt that this would be a great honor, not only for me but for my family as well. I looked forward to the challenge. This would be an opportunity to make my parents proud of me; it was an opportunity to exercise that new responsibility, of being the big brother who must set an example for his younger brothers and sister. Most importantly, it was an opportunity to bring something positive into what had become a very somber home.

There had never been any contact – that I was aware of – between my parents and the scout leaders before or after the funeral. I wondered what my parents' feelings were toward the scout leaders, but no clues were ever given by them. I think that my being a candidate for this award was an example of the scout leaders' reaching out to make a public statement that there was harmony between the scouting association and the family. Whether I saw the possible political implications at the time, I don't know.

It didn't matter to me why I was chosen because I knew I would have to earn it. This was my opportunity to do something special on my own. It would make me worthy of taking on those responsibilities that I felt were mine now that Loren was gone. As the older brother, I had certain responsibilities. I had to be to my brothers and sister what Loren had been to me. I felt that I had to earn, for myself, that same respect that I had given to Loren. I had to build a pedestal for myself that was just as tall as the one on which I had placed Loren. I had no idea what an impossible task that would come to be.

The aim of the *Ad Altare Dei* award was to recognize those First-Class Scouts who had served "with loyalty and fidelity" both their church and scouting. The purpose of the award was to equip the scout to take his place in the world as a maturing Catholic and a maturing American. Under the direction of a religious counselor, Leo and I would meet requirements blending scouting with religion. The requirements of the program were that we had to be at least a First-

Class Scout, a member of a registered troop, a resident within the diocese, and an altar boy for at least 250 hours completed. Among other things, we would have to demonstrate our ability to make all Catholic Mass altar responses in Latin. The pastor of our parish had to certify that the scout was worthy to receive the award based on punctuality, fitness, devotion, and decorum on the altar.

The first award of the *Ad Altare* Cross was in 1926 in the Diocese of Los Angeles. It wasn't until 1939 that approval was given to wear this emblem on the scout uniform. This was the first religious emblem ever approved to be worn on a scout uniform.

In order to earn the award, we had twenty-four requirements to meet during a two-month period. Weekly meetings took place in the office of Father Francis X. White at the church rectory. Father White was the assistant pastor of our church and the chaplain for Boy Scout Troop 24 of Queen of the Miraculous Medal Parish. Fr. White was the priest who had given Loren the Last Rites of the Catholic Church immediately after his body was recovered.

Father White was a dedicated priest, a great man who was loved by everyone. He nearly always had a smile on his face, and that smile could light up a room. He had been the home plate umpire at the annual seventh and eighth-grade baseball games for as long as I could remember. He was a very patient man and all of the altar boys looked forward to serving for him. Our mistakes as altar servers were not only overlooked, but sometimes even drew a mischievous smile from him.

Leo and I met with Father White once or twice a week, usually just after lunch. Sometimes Father White came into the office, where we met, still chewing the last bites of food. More often than not, he entered the room with his Roman Collar hanging loosely around his neck. I remember how odd that looked, not only because we seldom saw a priest without his collar in place, but also because he was so meticulously dressed otherwise, with his black shoes freshly shined to a high gloss, sharply-pressed black slacks and shirt. He was probably in his early fifties, about five foot ten, maybe 165 pounds and graying hair, a very distinguished looking man. I don't know whether it was intended or not, but the Roman Collar left askew made it a very relaxed setting for Leo and me.

Upon our selection for the award, Leo and I had been given a pamphlet that set out the subject matter to be covered in each session. Therefore, we knew in advance the subjects on which we would be questioned. We knew, for example, that a given session would cover such things as our being able to demonstrate the correct manner of making the Sign of the Cross, of genuflecting, or of greeting a bishop, priest, sister, and religious brother. We had to know the proper way to enter and leave a church, and the correct etiquette for attending Mass. We had to own and demonstrate the use of a Sunday Missal. We were expected to know the names of our bishop, pastor, troop chaplain, and diocesan chaplain. We were also required to explain how we would go about preparing a sickroom for the visit of a priest, how we would meet the priest and conduct him to and from the sickroom. Both Leo and I had attended Catholic school beginning in the first grade. Therefore, many of these items were second nature to us and were easily and eagerly answered.

Another session that I remember was not quite as easy. We were required to identify all of the vestments and other articles used at Mass. Leo and I got together to work on this one before our meeting with Father White. Even though we were both altar servers and dealt with the priests' vestments regularly, we were sure that a rehearsal was needed.

FR. FRANCIS X. WHITE C.M.

ASSISTANT PASTOR

1949 - 1957

When our next meeting with Father White arrived, we were ready. We knew that the vestments consisted of the alb, the cincture, the maniple, the stole, and the chasuble. We were also able to identify the articles used in the celebration of the Mass: the chalice, the paten, the ciborium, the purificator, the corporal, the pall, the chalice veil, and the burse.

Sometimes Father White asked us individual questions. For example, he would look at me usually with a smile) and say, "Dougie (I never told him that I hated the name Dougie), what is the name of the cloth that covers both the chalice and the paten?" I would answer, "That's the chalice veil, Father." He would smile his approval, then look at Leo and ask him a question. On occasion, Father White would expect both of us to answer together. This technique was most appreciated when it came to the Latin Mass responses.

It was one thing for Father White to say, "*Dominus vobiscum*," and expect a response of "*Et cum spiritu tuo*" from Leo or me. That was simple enough for altar boys to remember and pronounce individually. It was quite another matter when it came to the Confiteor. This prayer, Father White asked us to say together: "*Confiteor Deo omnipotenti, beatae Mariae semper Virgini, beato Michaeli Archangelo, beato Joanni Baptistae, sanctis Apostolis Patro et Paulo, omnibus Sanctis, et tibi Pater quia peccavi nimis cogitatione verboo, et opere: mea culpa, mea colpa, mea maxima culpa. Ideo precor beatam Mariam semper Virginem, beatum Michaelem Archangelum, beatum Joannem Batistam, sanctos Apostolos Petrum et Paulum, omnns Sanctos, et te Pater, orare pro me ad Dominum Deum*

Nostrum."[1]

Father White obviously knew the difficulty that prayer presented to most altar boys. He also knew if we said it together, we could cover each other's mistakes. When one of us stumbled over a word or two, the other's voice would muffle the mistake.

In addition to serving as our Boy Scout Chaplin, Father White was the priest who administered the Last Rights to Loren at the edge of the lake. During our meetings it became obvious that Loren was on his mind when Father unintentionally entered Loren's name, rather than mine on the pages that required signatures. Father White signed off each of these sessions as Leo and I successfully completed them. After two months of weekly meetings, Leo and I had received all of the appropriate signatures in our study booklets. The final step was to complete the requirements of moving from a Second-Class Scout to a First-Class Scout. This was to be the easy part; I only had one step left to complete the requirements to become a First-Class Scout. That final step was the swimming test.

One February evening in 1957, sometime after dinner, our phone rang. My mom or dad (I don't remember which one) answered it. I was told it was for me. When I came to the phone, I recognized the voice as our assistant scoutmaster, even before he identified himself.

---

[1] English translation of *Confiteor*; I confess to almighty God, to blessed Mary ever Virgin, to blessed Michael the Archangel, to blessed John the Baptist, to the holy apostles Peter and Paul, and to all the saints that I have sinned exceedingly in thought, word, and deed, through my fault, through my fault, through my most grievous fault. Therefore, I beseech blessed Mary ever Virgin, blessed Michael the Archangel, blessed John the Baptist, the holy apostles Peter and Paul, and all the saints, to pray for me to the Lord our God. Amen.

He was calling to tell me that I was late for the scout meeting being held that night at the Frost Elementary School's swimming pool. He went on to remind me that I needed to pass the swimming test as the final step in achieving my First-Class ranking.

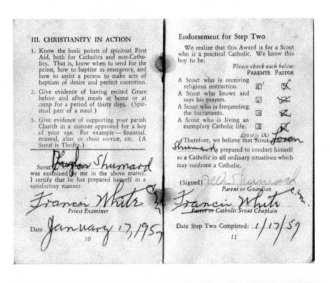

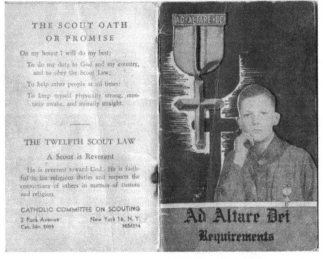

Our home was only a few blocks from Frost School. I told my scoutmaster I would be right there. I went upstairs to my room to grab a towel and find my swim trunks. As I began the search for my trunks, I began to feel an overwhelming fear, frustration, and anger. I didn't know why. I could feel an internal pressure so intense that I thought I was going to explode.

As I struggled to find my trunks, only half-seeing the contents of my clothes drawer, I remembered that since Loren had drowned I had avoided going near the water for any reason. Why had I avoided the water? I was never a good swimmer, never as good as Loren. In spite of the fact that Loren was a good swimmer, he had drowned. My thinking was that if my brother, a good swimmer, could die in the water, why should I ever go near the water?

I knew that the swimming test was only a single length of the pool, the same distance that I had to swim to pass a test at the local YMCA when Loren and I learned to swim just a couple of years earlier.

It didn't matter that the test was only the length of the pool, I knew I couldn't do it. Loren was a good swimmer and he had drowned. I was a poor swimmer; what was going to happen to me? How could I get into the water under the supervision of all of the same scout leaders who were there when my brother died?

I was becoming aware that by not going I would be throwing away all of my efforts toward achieving the medal. Worse yet, I would be disappointing my parents. I was trying to make them proud of me; I was trying to show them that they could be as proud of me as they had been of Loren. I had failed my brothers and sister in not being able to do everything that Loren did.

I was letting everyone down, and I had failed. I was one short, swimming pool lap away from completing the requirements for the *Ad Altare Dei* Award, and I was making the decision to throw it all away.

The explosion that I thought I felt earlier finally came. I began to cry, not just to cry but to bawl. I slammed the bedroom door as hard as I could. I threw things. The clock next to my bed was smashed to the floor, and the clothes in my drawers were scattered around my room. I was angry, and I was hurt. I was crying over the loss of the medal, and I was finally crying over the loss of my brother, and I was crying because I realized that I would never be able to fill Loren's shoes. I was crying like a baby, not like the big brother I was trying to become. I had failed my parents, my brothers and sister, and myself. I was, by then, fourteen years old, too old to cry and too young not to.

All of the noise that I was making brought my parents to my room. By then, I was crying uncontrollably, knowing that I was a total and complete failure. When they asked me what was wrong, I screamed some response about the swimming test, and that I just couldn't do it. My folks did their best to comfort me but they would never know the depth of my total despair at that moment. Although the crying finally stopped, the feeling of failure engulfed me totally.

Sometime later the phone rang again. I was still upstairs in my room when I overhead my mom talking. I could overhear enough of the conversation to know that it was my scoutmaster again. He was obviously explaining to my mom the importance of this swimming test as it related to the award. My mother told him that I would not be coming. I could hear the phone being hung up and at that moment I knew it was over. I had let everyone down, but most of all I had failed.

The respect that I had tried so hard to earn would not be mine. I realized that I would never be able to deserve, from my brothers and sister, that same respect that I held for my older brother. The pedestal on which I had placed Loren was unachievable. I never attended another scout meeting after that. I could see, only too clearly, my failures and I was sure that the other scouts and scout leaders knew them as well.

Leo Lyng completed all of his requirements, and Bishop Joseph H. Albers presented him the *Ad Altare Dei* Medal at Queen of the Miraculous Medal Church. I have no idea what I was doing that day or which Mass I attended, but I do know that I did not attend the award ceremony. I was happy for Leo. I knew better than anyone how hard he had worked for that award, and he deserved it.

One year later, Leo and I parted company. I moved on to St. John's High School while Leo chose to attend the crosstown rival, St. Mary's. Because we were attending different schools, we saw each other only at an occasional sporting event or possibly Sunday Mass. After high school, I went to Oklahoma to attend school. I never saw Leo again. I found out sometime later that Leo attended Central Michigan University where he majored in English and became a schoolteacher.

On August 12, 1966 Leo Lyng died. Leo was just 23 years old. While he was in college, it was discovered that Leo had cancer. He lived less than six months after the diagnosis. It had been four years since we had last seen one another and about ten years since we had worked with Father White on the *Ad Altare Dei* Medal.

Visit to the Place of Loren's Death

"Angels can fly because they take themselves lightly."
~G. K. Chesterton

As an adult, I occasionally thought about visiting the farm and the lake where Loren drowned. For many reasons, the thought was always short-lived, among other things. I left Jackson, Michigan, in my late teens and didn't return to the area for nearly thirty years. Even after I came back, when the thought of the visit returned, I realized that I had no idea of the location of that Boy Scout outing in 1954. As I indicated earlier, my parents never spoke of the event; therefore, I had absolutely no knowledge of where this place was located. Certainly, I had read and reread the newspaper's account many times over the years, and the address of the location was part of that article. Even though the address was available to me, I never connected that street address with an actual location, and the thought never crossed my mind that I could – or even should – visit the site.

During September of 2001, as I began to summarize my memories of this event, I once again reread the May 2, 1954, newspaper account of the drowning. This time I made a note of the address, in the second paragraph: "...the property of Douglas MacCready, 9124 Myers Rd., about 11 miles southeast of Jackson." I now had a burning desire to find that location.

With this bit of information in hand, I located my map

for Jackson County and reviewed the street/road index. There it was, Myers Road, near Clark Lake and only a few miles from the homes of relatives of both my wife and I. It had become obvious that I, unknowingly, had been within just a few miles of this site many times over the years.

Now what to do? I had a map. I was familiar with the area. It was less than a half-hour from my home. Was this something that I really wanted to do? Had I put it off all these years because I didn't know where to go, or did I not go because I really was afraid to go? I was about to find out.

As I drove south on Highway 127, I began to question my own judgment. What was this visit going to prove? It had been nearly fifty years; the farm would probably be a subdivision full of homes now. It struck me that nothing could be as it was in 1954, and Mr. MacCready must be long gone, either moved away or dead. *Oh well*, I thought, *I had come this far I might as well continue.* At that point, I realized that I was trying to talk myself out of this visit. I was beginning to feel that this might not be a good idea.

Continuing along the highway, I took a quick glance at the notes taken from my map: "South on 127 to Wetherby, take a right on Wetherby, then continue for a mile and left on Myers." There it was. There was Wetherby. I turned right and would soon come to Myers Road. It was too late to turn back now. I was pleased to see that this still was very much a country setting, some farms but mostly just single-family homes on 20 or more acres. I checked the addresses on the mailboxes along the side of the paved country road.

Finally, there it was, 9124 Myers Road. The mailbox

was on my left, but there was no sign of a building any place in sight, nor did it look like there could have ever been any building on that sort of lowland. As I looked to the right side of the road, the absolute beauty of what I saw overwhelmed me: acres and acres of green, lush lawn, magnificent huge trees of all varieties, colorful flower gardens scattered across the property, a narrow blacktop driveway leading from the road to the house. From what I could see from the car, it was like a trip back in time. It appeared as though this property could have looked just this way in 1954.

I drove by, very slowly a number of times, realizing that I had no real plan. Now that I was here, what should I do now? I couldn't just go up to the door, knock, and tell them that my brother died there nearly fifty years ago. I didn't even know who lived there now; the MacCreadys were probably long gone. Worse yet, if they were still there and I announced my reason for being there, it would probably be a terrible shock to them.

For whatever reason, the beauty of this place made me comfortable with my decision to be there. However, I was sure that I needed to rethink going any further than the road, at least for now. When I returned home, I went to the Jackson phone book to look up Douglas MacCready. Would he be listed at all? Would he still be at the Myers Road address? If not, then what? To my amazement, there he was, listed. *Okay, now what? How do I make contact? Do I drive by hoping to find him working in the yard? Do I phone him for a meeting?*

Months passed as I continued to occasionally drive past the Myers Road address. I weighed my options because I became convinced that this was the right thing to do. I not only wanted to visit the site, but I wanted to talk to Mr. MacCready about the event. The only knowledge that I had was of the newspaper account and I wanted — no, I needed — to talk to someone who was there, someone who could tell me more.

Finally in August 2002, nearly a year after my first drive-by of Myers Road, I decided to write Mr. MacCready a letter requesting permission to visit his property:

August 23, 2002
Dear Mr. MacCready,
I am in the process of preparing a Shumard family history for my younger brothers and sisters, for my wife, for my sons and my daughter, and my grandchildren. I find there is a significant part of the history that is incomplete. That incomplete portion revolves around the drowning of my older brother Loren, in 1954.

The reason for this note is to ask that you allow me to come to your property, to visit the site of my brother's death. By no means do I want to open old wounds. Rather, I want to take this step in order to gain a better understanding of that day nearly 50 years ago.

It is with the greatest respect and understanding that I ask this tremendous favor of you and your family.

You may reach me at the following phone numbers...

...and gave Mr. MacCready my home address and phone numbers. I knew that there was only a slight chance for any kind of response to my letter.

The letter to Mr. MacCready went in the noon mail on

Saturday August 24th.The following Monday at five p.m., my phone rang. The caller I.D. read, "Douglas MacCready."

After a brief conversation, Mr. MacCready and I agreed to meet the following morning at nine a.m. I was both grateful and surprised that Mr. MacCready would respond to my letter. I knew that this visit could be as potentially painful to him as it probably would be for me.

Through the years since Loren's death, there had never been any contact between our family and the MacCreadys. Even though Jackson is a relatively small town, our families, for whatever reason, never crossed paths. MacCready, after all, is not an uncommon name. In those cases when I may have heard a reference to that name, I never made any sort of connection. After the first drive-by of the Myers Road property, I paid closer attention when I heard the name or saw it in print.

I learned, for example, that in 1944, when Doug MacCready was just twenty years old, he started the Jackson Glove and Canvas Company. The business manufactured canvas gloves for the war effort. By 1950, his brothers, Lynn and Willis, joined Doug and the business became the Jackson Canvas Company. One of the many items produced was a slip-on canvas cover for lawn and garden tractors. The contacts formed by the MacCreadys with these major manufacturers of lawn equipment lead to the formation, in 1960, of a second company called the Michigan Seating Company. With the growth in the popularity of riding lawnmowers, this new company with the most highly automated plant in Jackson County, its 210,000 square foot facility, and 500 employees—became a leader in the manufacturing and sales of seats for garden tractors, lift tractors, construction, and agricultural equipment. As the MacCreadys were quoted as saying in the January 2002 issue of Jackson Magazine, "Any industrial equipment that has a seat on it, chances are, it came from us."

I also learned that the MacCready Brothers had donated over four hundred acres of the Myers Road property to Michigan State University, which would utilize the preserve for the education of forestry. From the article in the Jackson paper, "...the property is valued at $1.45 million and features glacial hills, small lakes and ponds, springs, streams, conifer and hardwood forests, wildflowers, an old orchard, and abundant wildlife. The brothers also donated $600,000 to create an endowment that will produce money to manage the property." Willis MacCready was quoted as saying, "A forester once told me this is the largest pine forest south of Houghton Lake."

As I made the twenty-five-minute drive to Myers Road, I questioned once again the wisdom of this visit. I wondered how I would react when I actually visited the small lake where my brother lost his life. I wondered how cordial Mr. MacCready would be. I wondered, if this was such a good idea, why did it take me fifty years to do it? I thought about the newspaper photo that appeared in the paper that Sunday morning after the drowning. That photo showed three firemen in a rowboat, about to launch from a small sandy beach. In the background, there were five or six adults who were in already on the lake in search for my brother's body. The event described in that newspaper story was why I had to make this visit.

The event that took so little space in a small-town newspaper played such a significant role in my life. I have always known that May 1, 1954, not only changed my childhood but also quite possibly changed who I ultimately came to be. I knew, for example, that when my brother died I felt compelled to take his place, to be to my brothers and sister what Loren had been to me. I had placed Loren on a pedestal and my eleven-year-old mind didn't know that I had gifted him with powers that he did not possess. Without knowing it, I was placing on my shoulders an unachievable set of responsibilities that would only add to my confusion and grief. For this reason, I had an absolute burning desire to learn as much as possible about the circumstances that so greatly changed my life.

The 1954 front-page story was the only version of my brother's death that was available to me. I wanted to talk to someone who had been there at that time; someone who knew the entire story. I know that a newspaper seldom conveys the entire story, and because of that, they may not always get it correct. I wanted – I needed – to know what my brother and his two friends were up to that day. How did they escape the supervision in charge of the scouts that afternoon? Did my dad ever contact the MacCreadys? Did he ever visit the site? I wanted small details. Where was the raft located that the three boys found and played on? How far away was the ballgame that the scoutmasters were supervising? How had the site changed since 1954?

Once again, I drove the twenty-five-minute trip. I exited I-94 and took 127 south about ten miles to Wetherby Road. A right turn on Wetherby and about a mile to Myers Road, left on Myers and after a short distance, for the first time, I turned into the driveway.

The driveway was single lane, paved, tree-lined with large boulders along both sides of the approximately 600-foot-long drive. As I approached the house, I noticed there were small ponds on both sides of the long driveway. The house was a very attractive ranch-style, built on a hill so that the garage was under the house where you would normally expect to find the basement. The entry to the garage was directly under the center of the home at basement level. My thought, once again, was that the house and property probably had not changed much since 1954.

Mr. MacCready met me at the door with a strong handshake and an invitation to join him for a cup of coffee. I estimated him to be about 80 years old; some twenty or thirty years my senior, he appeared to be about five foot six. He was deeply tanned and looked to be physically strong, with the build of someone who was regularly involved in outdoor activities.

Mr. MacCready was very personable and outgoing. Our conversation began with him telling me that he had recently returned from visiting his daughter and grandchildren at their home in Alaska. He was just beginning to show me photos of that visit when his wife joined us. She too was gracious and joined in our conversation.

Mrs. MacCready said that Doug's youngest daughter, during a visit within the last month, had brought up the drowning on their property back in the fifties. This daughter was eleven years old at the time and was playing outside when she heard a commotion, yelling, and screaming coming from the scout's camp area. Mr.

MacCready interrupted to point out that the yelling and screaming from the campsite was different. His wife went on to say that his daughter ran to the lake, saw the panic of the search, and raced back to the house to tell her father.

The MacCready Farm

Mr. MacCready told me that he has many times told the scout leaders that the lakes and ponds were definitely off-limits. He went on to tell me that scouts had used his property for camping on many occasions. He told me how he took great pleasure in the sounds of the boys enjoying their camping experience, the yelling during their ballgames, and the screams of delight when they spotted a deer racing across the field.

The screams that day, in 1954, were different. They were not screams of delight; they were screams of terror. Terror for a missing pal, terror for themselves because they had been doing something that they had been forbidden to do by their leaders.

I asked Mr. MacCready just how close the ballgame was to the lake where the boys had gone to find the raft. I asked him, if the game was close to the lake, and how could the scout leaders not be aware of the absence of my brother and his two friends? Mr. MacCready, for the first and only time that day, became slightly agitated and said, "There were no scout leaders. They had all gone into town to get hamburger meat for a cookout to be held later that day."

His statement stunned me: "...no one there, they had all gone into town to get hamburger meat!" The newspaper account of the drowning was very specific in stating that scout leaders "were directing a softball game in a nearby field." When I pointed this out to Mr. MacCready, he seemed to recant slightly and then held firm to the account that the leaders had gone to town, leaving the scouts alone. The only mention of the scout leaders not being present at the time of Loren's death were from Mr. MacCready, his wife, and daughter. I never heard that from anyone else.

We left the house through the back door and walked to the barn to begin our tour of the property. His barn was obviously a relatively new addition to the property. It was an all-metal pole barn, maybe forty x fifty feet with a concrete floor, an overhead door, and the service door through which we entered. The inside of the barn was a combination of storage, workshop, and retreat. There was a furnace against the back wall. Various animal heads were mounted and hung on all four walls. In the center of the barn was a John Deere Gator, a gas-powered utility vehicle that seats four.

Mr. MacCready raised the overhead door, and as I climbed into the vehicle, he fired up the engine of what was to be our morning's transportation. We immediately entered a well-worn path that just fit our four-wheel drive vehicle. It was obvious that this vehicle had been on this very path a number of times before. As we drove, Mr. MacCready pointed out various features of the property. One of the first things that he told me was that, at one time, he knew the names of most every plant and every tree on the 400-acre property. He told me that his mother was a great teacher in this regard, and that his first wife, who had died some years before, had picked up where his mother had left off and continued to educate him in the identification of the many varieties of vegetation on the property.

We toured the MacCready estate for nearly two hours, across miles of trails, through hundreds of acres of forests, lakes, streams, artesian wells, and the "largest stand of pine forest south of Houghton Lake." At one point we were looking down a steep ravine, a hill that extended for two to three hundred yards in front of and behind us. Mr. MacCready told me that this was the top of a formation of gravel. He was told a few years earlier that this potential gravel site was worth, "a king's ransom" and that he had turned down a significant offer that would allow the gravel to be quarried. He went on to tell me that he had refused because it would have completely changed the face of this lovely landscape forever.

In the midst of our conversation, the vehicle slowed and then came to a stop. We had arrived at a small lake. As I got out of the vehicle I noticed high weeds and deep underbrush to my right. I looked to the left where there were more weeds and underbrush mixed with trees. Only very faintly through the trees could I see a small lake. After a couple of steps, we were on a sandy patch of ground measuring about ten by fifteen feet. A small aluminum fishing boat was pulled onto the beach, completely out of the water.

As I gazed across this sandy patch, out into the lake, I remembered the picture on the front page of the newspaper from that Sunday morning, showing the firemen in the rowboat getting ready to push off to search for my brother's body. This was that exact spot!

The lake appeared to be four or five acres, nearly round, surrounded by both pines and hardwoods. With all of the grief that I still held, with the fear of water that had been with me all this time, with all of the baggage that had traveled with me through these many years, I was overwhelmed with, of all things, the beauty of this place. I was thinking of how ashamed I should be in seeing so much beauty in a place that I thought I should despise.

I stood close to the water's edge. Glancing down, I noticed a number of minnows flash by in the crystal-clear water. At that moment, I thought how odd it was that there could possibly be life in this place, which I had, for so long, associated only with death.

Mr. MacCready pointed to the spot where the raft, which the boys took out that day, was located. He told me that both he and a friend, who had been visiting that day, ran to the lake and swam out in search of Loren. I asked him to point out the nearby ball field where the other boys were playing. He turned one hundred and eighty degrees from where we were facing the lake and pointed in the direction of the weeds and underbrush that had been on my right as

110

we arrived at this spot. Over the many years that had passed, the ball field had become a field of weeds.

The weeds had taken over the ball field, fish were thriving in the lake, birds were chirping all around us, and thousands of magnificent trees surrounded us, some over fifty feet tall. Life has gone on here as though nothing of any consequence ever took place. How can personal tragedy affect us so deeply while the rest of the world goes on without taking notice?

This preserve, this site, this magnificent land, although virtually untouched through these nearly fifty years, had nonetheless changed. The ball fields, campsites, and hiking trails were overgrown with weeds and brush. They have returned to what they were before they were transformed into a ball field. They have returned to what they were before they were cleared for agricultural purposes. They have returned to nature.

We continued our journey. I had seen what I had come here to see. I had visited the place of my brother's death. I had spoken to someone who was there. I had learned some additional information. I had accomplished my mission. As we pulled away, I glanced to my left once more to see the sandy path and the lake. I thought again of the front-page newspaper photo as I said a silent prayer.

A Letter to My Father

"The failure to forgive can have a much more debilitating effect on the soul than what may have been a passing event and is now long finished."
~Fr. Donald Haggerty

My dad died in 1984 without the two of us ever having been able to discuss the issues that I write about on these pages. The following letter is some of what I would have liked to say to him:

Dear Dad,

After graduating from college in 1971 and relocating to the Chicago area and later back to Michigan with Barbara and our children, we were for the first time in ten years, able to visit with you in Jackson on most weekends. You and I were fortunate enough to finally become very close; I didn't know if it was because of my college degree, the wife I chose, or because of my children (your grandchildren). It was probably quite simply, that we had both changed over the years, both mellowed. For whatever reason, I felt that I had earned your respect and, most importantly, your love. We were close at that time and I savored the relationship.

You were not only a wonderful grandfather to my children, you were something of a hero to them. Many times I watched you and my sons in amazement, and maybe with a little envy, wishing that you and I could have been that close during all of our turmoil surrounding Loren's death, Mom's hospitalization, and

113

your terrible fear of losing another child. I needed you so badly and so simply. Just an arm on my shoulder, a soft word in my ear, something that would have told me that we are together, we are still a family, and that you would get me through this. Instead, none of us, you included, ever really did get through it.

Even during our close adult relationship, I never raised the subject of Loren's death. I suspect it was because for so many years the subject remained forbidden. Maybe it was that I just didn't want to cause you further pain, or maybe I didn't want to cause myself further pain. Maybe I was afraid I would open other issues that would look like I was casting blame on you, questioning your parenting skills, and increasing your pain and embarrassment. You were a very proud man and your son died while misbehaving, doing something that all of the scouts were told not to do. Then Mom, your wife, is placed in a mental hospital. You must have been working very hard either trying to get in touch with, or trying to bottle up, your own feelings.

In spite of all of that, I so wish I had taken that opportunity to talk to you and ask about Loren's death; to talk then, as we should have much earlier. I should have asked you to tell me all you knew about that period of time. I know how difficult it would have been for you to discuss it, and I know how difficult it would have been for me to hear it. I know how very, very difficult it is for me just to write this.

Also I would have asked you how you could face those scout leaders when you ran into them on the streets or in the stores of our relatively small town. How did you stand it, to see Loren's friends, fellow

114

scouts and scout leaders at Sunday Mass?

I would have asked you to tell me exactly what the scout leaders told you about how these three boys, as well as the others who were at the lakeside watching, could have been completely unsupervised. I would ask what you knew about the comment of Mr. MacCready, regarding the adult scoutmasters being away from the campsite when Loren and his buddies were in trouble. I would have asked if you ever expressed your gratitude to Loren's pals, John Dragonetti or Jim Dwyer, the two boys who were with Loren when the raft came apart and the three were thrown into the water. I wondered if you had ever thanked John Dragonetti for his attempt to save Loren.

Whether you did or did not, I thank them both now. I thank them for their friendship with Loren and I thank them for their courageous efforts to save him. I can only imagine the pain that Jim and John have suffered over these many years. I am sure that their pain was every bit as deep as our family's pain and I can only hope, and continue to pray to God, that they have found peace with this.

Dad, I have to ask you if those comments, printed in the newspaper of May 3rd, were really your comments. I ask you this because I have always felt those were not words that you would have used. You would never have used the phraseology, "His troop leaders have all done fine work with the boys and we know they are absolutely blameless in this tragic accident." That is not how my father spoke; those are words that you would never use in the same sentence.

Continuing on in the May 3rd article, you were also quoted as saying, of Loren's death, "...it was just one of those things, and we are so appreciative of the fine time Loren had in scouting." This quote is by far the most unbelievable, the most cold-hearted statement that could ever have been attributed to anyone. You were tough, hard, sometimes unreasonable, and very unforgiving. But NEVER would you have said of your son's death, "It was just one of those things."

As I review these newspaper articles fifty years later, it is obvious, at least to me, that most, if not all of the statements in that May 3rd article came from a Boy Scout Council press release. All of these statements are self-serving to the Scout Council and may or may not have been passed by my parents for review, but I am sure they were not spoken by you or approved by you. It was obvious to me, even then, that those were not your words. Those were the words of the Scout Council press release.

A key example of a carefully constructed press release is the closing statement of Mr. Montford Mead, Land 'O Lakes Boy Scout Executive: "…any accident is thoroughly studied to prevent its recurrence." Reread that statement and substitute the word "investigated" in place of the word "studied." Notice how the careful use of one word can remove all possibility of blame.

There is only one other question that needs to be asked: Is it possible that maybe, just maybe, no one was at fault? Could it have been "just one of those things" as was written in the May 3rd edition of the Jackson newspaper? Could it have been just one of those terrible tragedies that happen randomly? This may be an explanation that would satisfy some, but I am sure that you agree that it is one that is not at all meaningful to those of us who carry these memories with us.

116

Most importantly, Dad, the reason I write to you, is to tell you that I understand.

To tell you that it is finally all right, that I did get through it, and that I love you very much. As an adult, as a parent, I understand the difficulties of fatherhood, the sometimes-overwhelming responsibility of parenthood: raising children, providing for them, nursing them through illnesses, educational issues, and the many land mines of today's society.

There has never been an instruction manual for parenting. No one has ever been required to pass a test and obtain a license before being able to become a parent. I know that you came to parenting with baggage from your own broken home. Your mother abandoned you, your brother and your father, when you were about five years old. I know that you never finished school and that you left your job as a farmhand in New York, and then made your way to Michigan when you were about sixteen.

I know that I have made some of the same mistakes with my family that you made with yours. I can only hope that my mistakes were few in number and minor in consequence. I hope from the bottom of my heart, that my (now adult) children understand both the importance, and the freedom, to approach Barbara and I for understanding and direction.

In closing, I want to tell you how much I love you. I want to tell you how much I miss you, but more importantly, to tell you how much you and I missed by not having this conversation that I am trying to have now. I know we both would have been the better for it.

With All my Love and Respect,
Doug

More about Mom

Mom lived in Jackson her entire life and, therefore, had many friends and family members with whom she maintained contact. As I mentioned earlier, Dad passed into eternal life in 1984 at the age of sixty-four; and Mom decided that she would continue to live in the apartment that she and Dad moved into years earlier.

At about that same time, Barb and I began making plans for construction of a home in Chelsea, Michigan. That home was designed and ultimately built with separate living quarters, hoping that Mom would, at some point, join us. It consisted of a large bedroom, private bath, and kitchenette area. In 1994, Mom made the decision to leave the Jackson apartment and live with us. Her friends and relatives visited her in Chelsea, and Mom had her own car that provided the freedom to take visits to Jackson as often as she desired.

It was shortly after that when I began putting my thoughts together regarding my brother's death and its impact on our family. Mom knew I was working on this, and she ultimately asked me to let her read what I was putting together. I was hesitant that she might not be able to handle it, due to the little memory that she had been left with as a result of the shock treatments. She made it very clear that she not only wanted to read it but wanted to discuss it as well, in spite of the fact that she had experienced the death of her firstborn, the death of her mother, and the death of her memory. I had experienced the death of my hero.

The goodness that came from these many discussions, revolving around the newspaper articles and photos, was that Mom was grateful and relieved to have gained an understanding of those events through conversations with Barb and me.

In 2009, Mom approached Barb and me regarding her wish to look into moving to Vista Grande Villa, an assisted-living facility in Jackson. This was a wise decision because it placed her back in her hometown among all of her many friends. Mom was also close enough to Chelsea so that Barb and I and Mom's grandsons and great-grandsons could visit her on a regular basis. I'm not sure who enjoyed those get-togethers more, Mom or her grandsons.

Mom died in 2014, on the day before her ninety-seventh birthday, and about one hour after receiving the Last Rights of the Catholic Church.

She understood my desire to fly, begun in childhood and shared with Loren, and she was supportive of my enthusiasm for aviation, including my homebuilt airplane pictured here.

High Flight

"Oh! I have slipped the surly bonds of Earth
And danced the skies on laughter-silvered wings;
Sunward I've climbed, and joined the tumbling mirth
of sun-split clouds, — and done a hundred things
You have not dreamed of —
wheeled and soared and swung
High in the sunlit silence. Hov'ring there,
I've chased the shouting wind along, and flung
My eager craft through footless halls of air....

Up, up the long, delirious, burning blue
I've topped the wind-swept heights with easy grace.
Where never lark, or even eagle flew —
And, while with silent, lifting mind I've trod
The high untrespassed sanctity of space,
– Put out my hand and touched the face of God."

By: John Gillespie Magee, Jr.

Epilogue

"There are three things extremely hard:
steel, a diamond, and to know one's self."
~ Benjamin Franklin

As I began to write this during the winter of 2001, my only hope was to place on paper my memories of a very specific subject. I was writing this rather selfishly, writing it for me. I was writing this because of my NEED to write it, just to get it out. I placed it all on paper because this event played a part in defining my life, in defining me. I wanted to go back in time to closely examine those events of 1954 that had such a profound impact on me. I wanted to know more about who I am, even why I am who I am. This trip back in time was sometimes surprising, always interesting, and many times painful.

Pals from the beginning

123

Naturally, Loren's death in some ways affected who I am today. I had always admired Loren in his position as older brother. Older meant bigger (much taller than I), smarter (his school grades were much better than mine were), more talented (he could fix anything, was much better at sports). I was a very immature eleven-year-old about to be a very immature twelve-year-old. I held a very unrealistic, exaggerated view of a big brother's responsibility. I somehow felt that I had to be the same kind of a hero to my brothers and sisters as Loren had been to me. I was setting up an impossible task for myself, one that was destined for failure, and one that merely added to my confusion. Obviously, I did not realize what was taking place; what I did know was that I was confused and frustrated.

The confusion and frustration all came crashing down that February evening in 1957. That was the evening when I received the phone call to report to the school pool in order to pass the swimming test to complete the First-Class Boy Scout requirements. This was to be the final step in preparation for the receipt of the *Ad Altare Dei* Medal. That is when I realized that I couldn't carry it off. I had failed; I could never meet those false, phony, unrealistic, responsibilities that I had invented for myself.

The decision-making process became very muddled, because I was trying to make decisions based on my perception of what my brother would do. In this case, I knew for sure that my brother was a good swimmer and yet he died in the water. Not only that, I knew he died with these same boy scouts present and the same scout leaders in charge.

It would be a long time before I would go in the water again.

124

Now that I look back on giving up the *Ad Altare Deo* Award, it was a blessing in disguise. It forced me to begin to see that I couldn't be what I was not. As terrible as I felt at that time, I know I felt relief that I no longer had to carry that heavy weight on my shoulders. If I was to be any sort of leader to my brothers and sisters, it would have to come in its own time. Besides, when Loren was alive, l liked having an older brother, a leader to look up to, someone to admire and follow. With his loss, I could no longer be a follower or a leader without pain.

As I write this, I question if this really was about my attempt to show some sort of leadership skills to my brothers and sisters; or was it really intended for my parents as an attempt to provide something to them that they lost in Loren's death? If I could be more like him, would that make me more acceptable to them? After all, Loren was the firstborn; his first name came from my dad's revered uncle, while my name came from a complete stranger, an army general. Loren had always been much more capable, a better student, and much healthier than me. I had been in and out of the hospital a dozen times, with a number of serious illnesses. My parents had been through a great deal with my many illnesses, and now the death of their firstborn son. I may have felt the need somehow, in whatever small way, to try to take care of them — to make everything okay, both for them and for me.

I have often wondered in what ways my life would be different if Loren had not died. After all, he and I were separated by only fourteen months. Would we have been fierce competitors in sports? I didn't begin a serious college career until seven years after high school. Loren would probably have gone to college directly out of high school. I know how I would have felt about that. Would we have competed for the same girlfriends? Would Loren and I have competed for the woman who ultimately became my wife? After all, she was two years older than I was, and that makes her only one year older than Loren.

I share this with you not to make excuses, not to cast blame, not to vent, but to simply present to you what I found along my journey. Most importantly, I hope you gain some personal insight. I share this with you knowing that many of you need this examination as much as I did. There is no question that my brothers and sisters—even those born after 1954—were each touched, to varying degrees, by our brother's death. To this day, there are many scars on family members. It is up to all of us to examine our personal baggage, our own scars, in order for them to heal. It cannot be done alone. We must each be courageous enough to seek the assistance of others, be it family members, clergy, or psychotherapists.

It is my hope that our children, my adult sons and daughter, your adult sons and daughters, can read this and feel some of the pain of this family history, enough of the pain to realize that life is filled with tragedy of all sizes. Just as importantly, I want them to see that there is recovery. No matter WHAT happens, there is recovery, we can go forward. We can overcome, but it is not necessary that we forget. Life lessons must be remembered. No matter how much pain, no matter how much adversity you face, no matter how hopeless you feel, no matter how little understanding you are getting from those around you, with all of that, you still can recover. No matter the pain, no matter the sense of hopelessness, there is tomorrow.

The words, the support that I needed most during the trauma of my brother's death, would have been, "Everything will be all right. We will get through this." I was eleven years old, just a month and a half away from my twelfth birthday. My brother Dennis was eight, two and a half months away from his ninth birthday. The adults in the family were having a very difficult time dealing with their own pain and were unable to provide support for us to deal with our pain. All I wanted was for someone to hug me, to put their hand on my shoulder and say, "I know you are hurting but everything will be all right. We will get through this." Remember those words – We will get through this – use those words to assist yourself, as well as others, to get to the other side of pain.

In our case, that would never happen. Our father would not allow the subject to be discussed. Our mother, due to her deep depression and later, as a result of the shock treatments, was completely unable to remember the events much less discuss them. Family members were left to fend for themselves. We were left to define our individual grief and to find our own road to recovery. I had a number of friends in the neighborhood, at that time, who kept me involved in our usual, activities. Most importantly, I was fortunate to have my teachers, especially Sister Rose, to help me during this period. As an adult, it has been especially gratifying to have the opportunity for many open discussions with my mother, and to witness her, and my own, ability to grow from these conversations.

I was a married man before I was ever able to discuss

Loren's drowning with anyone. The first person I ever talked to about it was Barbara shortly after we were married. Even then, at the age of twenty-two, I felt great emotion in relating this story to my young bride. It was a mix of sadness, and both relief and freedom, to finally be able to talk. I remember how strange it felt to be able to discuss this subject. Strange because I had never been able to hold this conversation with my own parents, never able to discuss it at length with anyone. This may have been the first time I thought about putting all of this on paper. It would be 2001 before I began putting my thoughts on paper, and 2018 before I decided to complete what I had started seventeen years ago.

This writing was originally intended strictly for my benefit, my self-therapy. As I progressed, I realized that my brothers and sisters and my own children might gain from this effort. As I reach its conclusion, I hope there may be others who might gain something from this peek over my shoulder.

All of us have, at one time or another, asked why do I have to suffer? Why did this happen to me? Why me? Those are common questions asked when negative situations present themselves. We need an explanation; we demand an answer even when there is no possible way to arrive at one. Even though we have known from our childhood that there is right and wrong, good and evil, we are somehow demanding of an understanding of the source of our suffering. Seldom, if ever, do we enter into a search for the truth of the good that comes to us that we accept without question. It seems that the natural tendency is to blame God for the suffering that is thrust upon us and give ourselves total credit for the good that comes our way.

My wife Barbara reminded me, "As an adult, it is a primary responsibility to discover that the 'why' of the questions of our childhood has nothing to do with the child who is the bystander. Being grown up and mature means facing the truth about people in general and parents in particular, then resolving not to let those events not faced in childhood harm those around us. It requires forgiveness but goes further than that. Resolution of childhood issues means you take a giant look at yourself to understand your over-reactions of irritability, depression, anxiety, guilt, fear of closeness, fear of abandonment, clinginess, stubborn controlling behavior, or even being passively angry or dependent. As human beings, that list goes on and on. The point is to know who you are, in reaction to what happened and forgive yourself." In other words, you are not the cause of what has happened. Don't become involved in the "blame game." Don't ask yourself over and over again, what could I have said, what could I have done so that would never have happened. Therefore, forgiveness of yourself is as important as the forgiveness of those, who in some way let you down.

I do not believe that the experiences that I have related here make me unique in any way. Everyone on the face of this earth has or will face some level of tragedy be it illness, death, financial hardship, physical or mental handicaps, drug or alcohol addiction, to name just a few. Along with the many joys that life holds, we must understand the reality of those negative aspects of life without either living in fear of it, or letting it run or ruin our life. Our responsibility is to let these experiences draw out the best in us, as some might say, to make lemonade out of lemons.

Each of us are put on this earth with the responsibility to leave some footprint, some sign that we were here. We must, even if in the smallest way, make this a better place, not only for ourselves, but also for those who follow. Some are gifted with the ability to influence the masses by their examples set in sports, industry, business, government, education, or religion.

Regardless of our position in society, we each have the power to effect and change the outlook and attitude of family, strangers – both adult and children – that we meet each day. The simple gesture of a nod, a smile, and a kind word as we pass is often all that it takes. Every day, we all create memories for those around us; why not make them positive memories?

An examination of our life can be compared to putting a jigsaw puzzle together. If we look deeply into ourselves, we can identify many of those individual pieces. Putting those pieces together is very difficult because, like all puzzles, the pieces don't always fit as easily as it might first appear. Some are easier to identify than others. Some are not only difficult to find but appear to be missing until the puzzle is nearly completed. While the completion of the puzzle is always difficult, there is a great deal of satisfaction in its completion.

During your personal journey, you will experience that there is a huge difference between learning from the past and dwelling on or living in the past. Learning from the past is critical; living in the past, in denial, is terminal.

One of the things I most enjoyed during my years in Oklahoma was the great heritage of the state and its people. When I arrived in Tulsa in 1962, nearly every place I looked, there was a reference to, "Tulsa—Oil Capital of the World." This was not a local slogan or a corporate exaggeration; it was a fact, not only at that time, but for most of the 20th century. Imagine the world's oil capital right here in Middle America. How times have changed.

I was also impressed with the ongoing respect for the state's rich Indian heritage possibly best expressed in the Oklahoma State flag that honors more than sixty groups of Native Americans. Additionally, there continues to be the access to Indian art, villages, and folklore. I learned of the many tribes that made their way to the Oklahoma Indian Territory in the 1800's. Many eastern Native American Tribes were forcibly removed from Indian Nations in Georgia, North and South Carolina, Virginia, Kentucky, and Tennessee. Cherokees made up one of the largest tribes to be relocated.

This relocation was under the direction of military troops, over the course of many months and much of it taking place during bitter winter weather. These conditions led to much suffering, hunger, disease, exhaustion, and many Indian deaths. This path that led them away from their homeland and resulted in such suffering became known as, "The Trail of Tears."

I relate the Indian heritage as background to a piece of advice that was repeated to me many times during my time in Oklahoma; a familiar story, that has also made the rounds on the Internet in recent years, and it reads as follows:

Two Wolves: A Cherokee Legend

An old Cherokee is teaching his grandson about life.
"A fight is going on inside me," he said to the boy.
"It is a terrible fight and it is between two wolves. One is evil – he is anger, envy, sorrow, regret, greed, arrogance, self-pity, guilt, resentment, inferiority, lies, false pride, superiority, and ego." He continued, "The other is good – he is joy, peace, love, hope, serenity, humility, kindness, benevolence, empathy, generosity, truth, compassion and faith. This same fight is going on inside you - and inside every other person too."

The grandson thought about it for a minute and then asked his grandfather, "Which wolf will win?"

The old Cherokee simply replied, "The one you feed."

Food for Thought
Prayers and Hymns

Amazing Grace
Amazing Grace, How sweet the sound
That saved a wretch like me
I once was lost, but now am found
T'was blind but now I see

T'was Grace that taught my heart to fear
And Grace, my fears relieved
How precious did that grace appear
The hour I first believed

Through many dangers, toils and snares
We have already come.
T'was grace that brought us safe thus far
And grace will lead us home,

Amazing grace, How Sweet the sound
That saved a wretch like me
I once was lost but now am found
T'was blind but now I see
Was blind, but now I see.

On the night before He died, Jesus said:
Do not let your hearts be troubled.
You have faith in God;
have faith also in me.
In my Father's house
there are many dwelling places...
If I go and prepare a place for you,
I will come back again
and take you to Myself,
so that where I am
you also may be...
Peace I leave with you;
My peace I give to you...
Do not let your hearts
be troubled or afraid. **(John 14:1)**

Memorare
Remember, O most gracious Virgin Mary, that never was it known that anyone who fled to thy protection, implored thy help, or sought thine intercession was left unaided.

Inspired by this confidence, I fly unto thee, O Virgin of virgins, my mother. To thee do I come, before thee I kneel, sinful and sorrowful. O Mother of the Word Incarnate, despise not my petitions, but in thy mercy hear and answer them. Amen.

Prayer of Saint Francis
Make me a channel of your peace
Where there is hatred let me bring your love
Where there is injury, your pardon Lord
And where there's doubt, true faith in you
Make me a channel of your peace
Where there's despair in life let me bring hope
Where there is darkness, only light
And where there's sadness ever joy
Oh, master grant that I may never seek
So much to be consoled as to console
To be understood as to understand
To be loved as to love with all my soul
Make me a channel of your peace
It isn't pardoning that we are pardoned
In giving to all men let we receive
And in dying that we're born to turn around
Oh, master grant that I may never seek
So much to be consoled as to console
To be understood as to understand
To be loved as to love with all my soul
Make me a channel of your peace
Where there's despair in life let me bring hope
Where there is darkness, only light
And where there's sadness ever joy

No Matter How Fragile I Feel, God is Breathing Within Me Now

Heavenly Father,

Hear my cry in darkness. I long for release from this mental oppression. You created me to be of worth and service. Help me now to break these ties of darkness that mutilate my soul. Touch my sins, real and perceived, and the sins of those who have harmed me, and release us from their wounding shame. Let your Holy Spirit enter into the lowliest of places in my heart and guide me from their prison, for I cannot alone find my way out. Grant me the strength to resist further harm to myself or others. Release me and restore my soul so that I may no longer buckle under the weight of these burdens. Only you can set me free from the crippling pull of these scars. For though this world may have demanded more of my body and spirit than you had ever intended, you my Lord can rebuild me. Heavenly Father, into your mercy and into your hands, I place my darkness and sorrows. Only you can make me well enough. Release me, Father, and quiet my anguish. Amen.

Margaret Rose Realy, Obl. O.S.B., 2008, Reprinted with permission.

Poetry

YOU

When I'm sick,
You stroke my brow,
When I'm learning
you show me how,
When I'm hungry,
you feed me too,
God's helping hand
is sent through you.

He sent you here
that I might live,
Not as an empty shell
or open sieve,
But that I might do
what he wants me to,
And that can't happen
Without you.
Helen Clark Shumard

I'm Free

Don't grieve for me, for now I'm free
I'm following the path God laid for me,
I took His hand when I heard Him call
I turned my back and left it all.
I could not stay another day
to laugh, to love, to work or play.

Tasks left undone must stay that way
I found that place at the close of day.
If my parting has left a void
Then fill it with remembered joy.
A friendship shared, a laugh, a kiss.
Ah yes, these things, I too will miss.
Be not burdened with times of sorrow.
I wish you the sunshine of tomorrow.
My life's been full, I savored much,
Good friends, good times,
A loved one's touch.
Perhaps my time seemed all too brief,
Don't lengthen it now with undo grief.
Helen Clark Shumard

Quotations

Denial ain't just a river in Egypt. ~Mark Twain

The credit belongs to the man…whose face is marred by dust and sweat and blood, who strives valiantly…and who, at the worst, if he fails, at least fails while daring greatly, so that his place shall never be with those cold and timid souls who neither know victory nor defeat. ~Teddy Roosevelt

After crosses and losses, men grow humbler and wiser. ~Benjamin Franklin – *Poor Richard's Almanac*

Every path has a few puddles. ~Will Rogers

You can clutch the past so tightly to your chest that it leaves your arms too full to embrace the present. ~Jan Glidwell

Life is tough; you must fight it out with hard work and perseverance to come out on the top. It doesn't matter how many times you are knocked down, what matters is how many times you get up. ~Paraphrasing General George A. Custer

We must become the change we seek in the world. ~Mahatma Gandhi

Don't be afraid to get frustrated. Look at me, I take a lot of Maalox. Somebody said to me not long ago, 'I'm surprised that a woman of such great faith would have to take Maalox.' I said, 'My friend, my stomach doesn't know about my great faith.' ~Mother Angelica

Be at War with your Vices, at Peace with your Neighbors, and let every New-Year find you a better Man. ~Benjamin Franklin, Poor Richard's Almanac

Notes
More History of Jackson, Michigan in 1954

As a delivery boy, I sometimes scanned the paper before doing my route. The Communist "scare" was all around us. The Army McCarthy Hearings were well under way in Washington, D.C. As an eleven-year-old, I understood what a senator was, but I wasn't too sure just what a senate hearing was all about.

Our hometown, Jackson, Michigan, population around 50,000, encompassed approximately ten square miles and had a total of eight air-raid sirens scattered around our normally very quiet city. These sirens were tested each Saturday at noon, with a three-minute wail followed by three one-minute blasts as an all-clear. Occasionally these sirens were tested during the week. If we were in school, we were instructed to take cover by placing our heads under our school desks. Even then, it seemed like maybe this wouldn't be much help during a nuclear blast, but we were kids, so what did we know?

As a county, we were concerned about the Communists generally and the Russians specifically. One of our prayers after each Mass ended with, "and save us from Russia."

In early 1950, then-candidate Dwight David Eisenhower campaigned in Jackson, the birthplace of the Republican Party. What a thrill that was for the city, as well as for me. I remember visiting the park where he spoke. I listened to his speech and then made my way to the back stairway leading to the speaker's platform. He was only a foot or two away from me when he came down, he was close enough for me to ask for an autograph, but I was too tongue-tied and couldn't get up the courage to ask. His slogan was "I like Ike" and it caught on quickly and was seen on hats and on buttons that could be pinned to our clothing. He was a popular general who was respected by most everyone at home during World War II. It just seemed natural that after the war, he would become a presidential candidate.

The visit by "Ike" was certainly a thrill, but it didn't hold a candle to the visit, some months earlier, of my real hero Gene Autry (and his horse Champion). The appearance took place at the Jackson County Building Auditorium, and it looked like every kid in the state was there. Gene sang all my favorites including, "Back in the Saddle Again," "Frosty the Snowman," "You are My Sunshine," and "That Silver-Haired Daddy of Mine."

Although I was thrilled to be there, I wasn't happy with my seat, so I somehow worked my way backstage. By the time the show was over, I was in a perfect spot to see Gene as he left his dressing room on his way outside. He looked very deserving of the hero status that I had bestowed on him. He was dressed in a camel-colored overcoat, a matching western hat and black cowboy boots, with the pants legs tucked into the boots (of course).

If you were in the market for clothing, you could buy a new suit for between $35 and $59 that you could pay it off in "ten easy payments." A pair of shoes to go with that new suit would set you back just $3.

You could buy a brand-new car for less than $2,000 from a wide choice of dealers: Ralph Lewis Studebaker on Pearl Street, Ordway Hudson, Kaiser and Willy's on

Prospect, O'Rourke Packard on Spring Arbor Road, Willard Nash on Greenwood, Clem Davis Ford on E. Michigan Avenue, Crutchfield Chevrolet on Jackson Street, Butler Buick on Pearl, along with many used car lots.

Gasoline was only 26¢ a gallon.

If you went to the grocery store, you could find bread at 18¢ a loaf and oranges at 45¢ a dozen. A candy bar was only a nickel and so was a Coke.

The movies were still a favorite of ours. There were six theaters in Jackson in the 1950s: the Michigan, Capital, Majestic, Rex, Family and Bon Ton. The latest rage was "Cinemascope" and "The Wonder of Stereophonic Sound," all for the kid price of just 35¢.

The United States flag had only forty-eight stars; Alaska and Hawaii were not yet states.

It would be another three years before a satellite named Sputnik would capture our imagination.

Area codes were unheard of; if we wanted to call long distance we dialed the operator and she placed the call for us.

A first-class postage stamp was 3¢.

Median family income was $16,000 a year.

Gold was $35 an ounce in 1954; today it is over $1,300 an ounce.

In the fifties, the newspaper radio listings were twice as large as the TV listings. Radio personalities included Jack Benny (with my favorite character Rochester), Our Miss Brooks (my favorite character was Walter Denton), and Edgar Bergan with everybody's favorite, Charlie McCarthy. For real excitement, there were Gangbusters, The Shadow, and Suspense Theater. On more than one occasion I was forbidden to listen to these last three shows because they were too violent. I guess some things never change, even in the days of radio there were concerns about violence.

The first television set in our neighborhood was just down the block. What a thrill it was to watch it for the first time. The picture was black and white, of course, on a round screen that was only about six inches across. Television reception was very grainy (snowy, we called it) and had a tendency to roll. Most of the first shows that I remember watching were on the Dumont Television Network and were only fifteen minutes in length.

The first television show that I ever saw was a program called Kukla, Fran, and Ollie. Fran was the only real person of the three. Both Kukla and Ollie were puppets. Every episode always seemed to have a theme, a sense of right and wrong, something to learn from this fifteen-minute show. Howdy Dowdy soon came along and then a number of my radio favorites made the transition to TV: The Lone Ranger, Burns and Allen, Jack Benny, and Ozzie and Harriet. The Colgate Palmolive Pete Hour featured Abbott and Costello on one Saturday evening and Martin and Lewis on the next Saturday night.

Photo Credits

Randolph St. (home), Family Photo.

Fr. John H. Dougherty, C.M (Fr. Doc), Queens Parish Photo.

Dennis, Doug, Loren, Family Photo.

Loren wins coaster race, Jackson Citizen Patriot, 6/29/53.

Doug with his car, Jackson Citizen Patriot, 6/25/53.

Front page headline and story, Jackson Citizen Patriot, 5/2/54.

Newspaper Article May 3, 1954, Jackson Citizen Patriot, 5/3/54.

Loren at Scout camp, Family Photo.

Loren, Family Photo.

Doug (newsboy), Jackson Citizen Patriot, 8/6/54.

Mom, Doug, Dad, Family Photo.

Sister Rose, Queens School Photo.

Ad Altare Dei, Doug's Photo.

Fr. Francis X. White, Queens Silver Jubilee Photo, 6/24/59.

MacCready Property, Doug's Photo.

Doug & Loren (forever pals), Family Photo.

State of Oklahoma, Statistics from Wikipedia, accessed 11/2002, https://en.wikipedia.org/wiki/Oklahoma

Native American India Story, Native American Legends, First People website, accessed 11/2002, https://www.firstpeople.us/FP-Html-Legends/Legends-AB.html

Mom, Doug and airplane, Barb's Photo.

Jackson Michigan Statistics, Newspapers and yellow pages from 1954.

Mercywood Hospital facts and figures, Ann Arbor News 6/11/72.

About the Author

Doug was born and raised in Jackson, Michigan. He attended Queen of the Miraculous Medal School from first through the eighth grade, and then St. John High School.

Not long after graduation, he enrolled in an aeronautical trade school, located in Tulsa, Oklahoma. He knew he wanted to become a pilot, and also knew he couldn't afford flight lessons. Instead, he enrolled in aircraft mechanic training, which was something he could afford. A short time later, he was able to begin pilot training in Tulsa, Oklahoma, where he earned a commercial pilot's license, followed by three additional licenses: instrument rating, a multi engine, and flight instructor.

After his marriage in 1964, he and wife, Barbara, made Tulsa their home. During this time he worked from dawn to dark as a flight instructor; flying during the day, and teaching ground school in the evening.

Doug, from the time he laid in the summer grass with his brother Loren, wanted to be a pilot, especially with the United States Air Force. Because he didn't have a college degree, he was never able to achieve this longtime goal. But in 1967 he was offered a position as civilian flight instructor in an Air Force pilot training program. This meant that he would be training Air Force officers, both in the air and on the ground, a great opportunity and a wonderful experience.

All of the students that were assigned to the training facility came from nearby Vance Air Force Base, Enid, Oklahoma. During that time, the first six civilian astronauts had been chosen by NASA, two of them assigned to train under Doug's group: Joseph Allen Ph.D. in Physics, along with Karl Henize Ph.D. in Astronomy. After completing their training, they both spent time as astronauts. Dr. Allen completed 127 orbits of the earth in 192 hours. Dr. Henize completed 126 orbits in 188 hours in space.

Doug's wife Barbara had earned a Master's Degree in Social Work from the University of Michigan in 1964, while Doug had decided that college was not for him. After working with Air Force officers who were all college graduates, he decided that it was time. He was accepted by the University of Oklahoma and graduated in three years by attending summer school, along with a fairly heavy workload and a dedicated wife.

After graduation from the University of Oklahoma, Doug was hired by Ford Motor Company as a marketing analyst. He and his family returned to the Midwest, where he worked serving first in the Chicago area and later in both Dearborn, and Detroit, Michigan. He retired after nearly thirty years at Ford.

Over the years, he and his family have lived in three states—Michigan, Oklahoma, and Illinois—and nine cities and have therefore been members of nine Catholic parishes. Doug has been a member of three parish councils: St. Mark's, Wheaton, Illinois; St. Kenneth, Plymouth Michigan; and St. Mary, Manchester, Michigan, where he also served as President of the council. Doug and Barbara are currently members of St. Catherine Laboure Parish in Concord, Michigan.

Doug Shumard is one of the founding members of Good Shepherd Catholic Radio, broadcasting from Jackson, Michigan, and is associated with Eternal Word

Television Network (EWTN) and Ave Maria Radio families.

He is a member of the Jackson, Michigan, Knights of Columbus Council 9131.

He and his wife, Barbara have three adult children, and will celebrate their 55th wedding Anniversary in September 2019.

CPSIA information can be obtained
at www.ICGtesting.com
Printed in the USA
BVHW03s2029051018
529422BV00001B/11/P